THE
PRINCIPAL'S
OFFICE

A NOVEL

THE PRINCIPAL'S OFFICE

An Inside Story

Barbara Ruben

Copyright © 2011 by Barbara Ruben.

Library of Congress Control Number:		2011917351
ISBN:	Hardcover	978-1-4653-7081-5
	Softcover	978-1-4653-7080-8
	Ebook	978-1-4653-7082-2

This book was printed in the United States of America.

To order additional copies of this book, contact:
Xlibris Corporation
1-888-795-4274
www.Xlibris.com
Orders@Xlibris.com
104329

For my sister, Tina

September 2007

Oh, Mrs. Ruben!

Perhaps we see clearest in a storm, in which case, though I find this decision troubling, I'll trust that your choice was the prudent one. Initially, this parting gift was to be a bottle of wine, a tangible evidence of both my thanks and good wishes. But not knowing if you like wine and, further, not trusting my own acumen in selecting a good vintage for the occasion, reflection and the gods led instead to this journal—a commonplace book in the waiting. My hopes are that the following pages will be filled with sundry recollections and conclusions drawn from your many good years here, all preliminary to the difficult, meaningful endeavor of turning out that book you plan to write. Your demeanor and inspiration have been of inestimable and profound value. The student forums, the liaison roles, the Consumer Smarts Senior Summit, and of course, the Harvard Model Congress have been changed for the better, largely through your energy and support. The awards ceremony and commencement were never as dignified or meaningful until you arrived. Enough of your space has been consumed by my maudlence (if that's a word!). I don't like change, Mrs. Ruben, but I understand that no one can step in the same river twice. The task of writing now falls to you.

Mr. Iannotti

PROLOGUE

Once, at a faculty meeting, I asked teachers to think about a teacher they had when they were in school and what emotion it evoked. All of them immediately recalled someone, and they all had vivid emotional recollections; some were for the better, some for the worse. The experiences attached to these memories were seared in the fabric of their lives.

Being sent "to the principal's office" more often than not conjures up unpleasant memories, and the principal is almost always associated with punishment—the rod, the ruler, the paddle—the one who has the authority to pass judgment. It is an archaic model and one we should rid ourselves of for the sake of our children. As Jonathan Kozol so aptly termed it, there are "savage inequalities" in public school education. Although the case can be made for socioeconomic conditions that breed good schools versus bad ones (higher performing versus underperforming), every parent and every child recognize the difference between excellence and mediocrity. Every parent and every child know what it feels like to be respected or humiliated. And every parent and every child recognize what it means to experience success and what it means to experience failure.

I have lived and worked in impoverished communities and in very affluent communities. Both have produced excellent educational experiences, and children have flourished. The answers have less to do with money and more to do with good leadership. In the hierarchy of the school system, leadership begins with the teacher who is supported, ideally, by the principal who is supported by the superintendent who is supported by the Board of Education that is supported by the community. If there is a single person along that chain in a position of power (teacher, principal, superintendent, board member) who is counterproductive to the vision and mission of providing excellent education for each child, everyone will bear the consequences. The longer the "weak links" are tolerated—whether by unions, complacent parents, board members, or school administrators—the health of the school institution is at risk. In assessing the health of an organization, it is easy to identify the weak links, and no doubt, many within the system are acutely aware of them. The vertical structure of the hierarchy precludes the necessary honest open dialogue and exchange. The education system deliberately lags behind, resistant to a new template that fosters (and rewards) excellence and promotes competition. It is designed to protect, even provide a safe harbor, for those who are not capable of leadership.

Good teachers—excellent, hardworking, dedicated, innovative, brilliant teachers—and administrators are held hostage by the promise of "future" security in pensions and health benefits. Yet they are the glue that binds the weak links together. They have the power because of their individual special talents and skills to teach, to demand working conditions and support, aligned with what they deserve, and they deserve to be extricated and disassociated from the weak links. Where is the outrage? What, by example, are we teaching our kids?

This book fictionalizes common, everyday school experiences both in regular public schools and alternative schools that address adolescents who have failed in the traditional system. This very fragile population is growing as conditions worsen within the family structure and the economy. These students, at fifteen or seventeen, after years of failure and abuse, are already angry, defeated, and hopeless. If the solution in an alternative setting is to give them more of the same, it is as costly to taxpayers as it is futile. Every day, extraordinary teachers, administrators, and support staff enter school buildings and do incredible work. It would not occur to them to arrive unprepared or late or unprofessional in their approach to their work. Their passion to teach, to engage students in the art and activities of learning, is powerfully visible.

Early on in my career as a principal, I met a grandmother who was raising her grandson whose father had died and whose mother had abandoned him. She came to every Back to School night, supported every school event, attended every board meeting, and persistently met every challenge (and there were many) of seeing this grandchild through adolescence and into adulthood. During one particularly tense period for me, as a new administrator, she bore witness to the upheaval caused when the stagnant waters of stale teaching were being stirred. The five words of encouragement she told me have been a guide for knowing, whatever the odds, that I was on the right track, and they have never failed. "Barbara," she said, "always look to the kids."

Laura Christler sits rigidly on the visitor's chair next to her bed, her long fingers nervously smoothing out the unwrinkled polyester of her brown skirt and rechecking the brass buttons on her turquoise jacket. Her face is pale, and the pencil-thin line of coral lipstick she applied an hour ago runs into the fine lines around her pinched mouth. "Just be patient," she admonishes herself. "You've waited this long, you can start over in a new place where no one knows you." Her head snaps up out of her reverie, and her watery blue eyes dart upward through her frameless spectacles as the aide enters the room.

"It's time to go now, Laura, Dr. Malone is ready to see you."

Laura stoops to pick up her paisley-print bag containing the few allowable personal items she has and follows the aide obediently down the fluorescent-lit long white corridor, past the glass-enclosed tech station with its red and green blinking lights and cacophony of bell tones and buzzers. The aide swipes her key card in the heavy metal doors, and they enter a separate hallway of hushed office suites and head toward the dark mahogany doors at the very end.

CHAPTER ONE

I remember my elementary principal, Mr. Carey. He was very tall and thin, always dressed in a suit, white shirt, and tie. He had a kind smile and a commanding voice. He was occasionally seen in the halls or at the doorway of the main entrance where buses disgorged a fairly respectful load of children. Other than that, at the end of sixth grade, he sat on the stage and presented certificates to awkward children, mine now somewhere faded under glass in a box in the attic labeled Barbara.

There were several principals in high school: Mr. Fox, Mr. Bouchain, and Mr. McFarland. All men. Since I was an honor roll student, my mother served on the Board of Education, and it was the decade spanning the '50s through the mid-'60s. I caused no reason to be summoned to the principal's office, as that would not have been a good thing.

I had exceptional teachers; it was, in fact, an exceptional school district. Bedded in the Catskills, two hours north of New York City, a community of one-room schoolhouses were consolidated to build a "central" school. Drawing students from the hills and hamlets within a five-hundred-square-mile radius, the communities (comprised of a feed store, produce market, and post office) borrowed their names from local Indian folklore. When the new "centralized" school opened its doors in 1952, it was a palatial edifice with terrazzo floors and glistening hallways. The library was hushed and filled with new books and smooth creamy-blond wood furniture. The cafeteria served hot lunches, cooked in a gleaming industrial kitchen by women who wore hairnets and spooned out generous portions of homemade split pea soup, mashed potatoes, baked chicken, and green beans. In all my years at school, I never saw a principal in the cafeteria. His office door was identified with a shiny brass plaque that read Principal and was always closed. Mine was the first class to attend kindergarten and go straight through to the twelfth grade. In 1965, as I proudly walked down the aisle of the twelve-year-old auditorium, never in my remotest dreams did I imagine I would return thirty-four years later as the principal of the same building.

The decade change from the '50s to the '60s was a yawn between a deep and comfortable sleep and being jolted fully awake by a raucous three-ring circus. A young man with long hair and jeans had already made an appearance at my house to discuss surveying some property for his house with my father.

When his lawyer, who accompanied him, introduced him to my father, he said, "Dan, you've heard of Bob Dylan!"

To which, my father replied, "Well, I've heard of a Matt Dillon from *Gunsmoke*, but no Bob Dylan."

But I had heard of Bob Dylan and Peter, Paul, and Mary, and knew every lyric Joan Baez and Judy Collins ever wrote. John Kennedy signs polarized the sleeping conservative community, and we were teens equally comfortable with black skirts, black tights, and black turtlenecks as we were fascinated by pillbox hats, empire-waist A-line sheaths, and the overall majesty and style of Jacqueline Kennedy.

The world to a college freshman at Boston University unfurled endlessly—offering course after course selection in liberal arts. Inspired by my high school English teacher, I plunged into the writings of the great masters—Chaucer, Spencer, Milton, and Yeats.

How deliciously comfortable to study art for art's sake—to sit on the steps of the Boston Public Library and study church spires in Copley Plaza for a humanities paper or stroll the Isabella Gardner Museum and see a real

Rembrandt. So much to learn and explore. Such oblivion to the changing times, such ignorance of the civil rights movement. Coming from my white rural school with my white teachers, my white family, my white community—my protected, sheltered, white-bubble life. "Here is your ticket to go to college," my mother would say. "Study liberal arts and marry a Harvard guy. Be a teacher—that's secure. Be ed-duu-cated."

Junior year, enrolled in the College of Liberal Arts and a declared English major, I minor in education. My first field experience is at an elementary school in South Boston, the same upon which Jonathan Kozol based his book *Death at an Early Age*. I arrive at my assigned second grade class with at least twenty or more black children. The teacher is white. The white principal enters the room, and in retrospect, I don't know why.

As though they practiced it in a principal-comes-to-the-room drill, twenty second graders stand and say in unison, "Good morning, Mr. Wilson."

To which he bellows, "I did not heeeaarrr you, so repeat that again!"

The children soberly and anxiously stand again, elevated voices, and say, "GOOD MORNING, MR. WILSON."

To which, he replies, "*Thaaat's* better!"

Mr. Wilson then begins a math lesson. (Why is the principal conducting a math lesson? I'm here to see the teacher.) He fires question after question to students, ridiculing unfortunate victims who stammer and blurt out wrong answers. I am immediately uncomfortable—outraged at his humiliating tactics—but sit, flush faced, like a good girl. I share the same fear as the second graders. Will he call on me, and will I be wrong? I leave the dilapidated and stifling neighborhood and catch the MTA to Back Bay. My field observations continue for six weeks. I learn the children's names and learn their stories; we fall in love. At Christmas, when I am home on break, I lie across the bottom of my parents' bed and read in a choked voice the letters they have each written and presented to me on my last day. I am twenty years old—brought to my knees by second graders who, quite simply, thanked me for my kindness.

As a senior, my student teaching assignment is at a middle school in Lexington, Massachusetts. I'm part of an innovative teaching team, a collaborative group of young teachers developing and implementing an interdisciplinary curriculum in humanities. It is 1968, and I am teaching a poetry unit. Students can select lyrics from their favorite songs and bring in their own guitars to sing them or write their own. The school glistens, the colors are bright, the classrooms are open, and the psychological aura is anti-spirit-crushing.

I have never seen the principal of this school. I do not know who he is, nor do I give him a thought. This is my student teaching assignment, and it is the teachers and my BU professor to whom I am responsible. I marry my Harvard guy shortly after graduation and move to a tiny town in Idaho where his parents manage a 2,300-acre potato farm. We will spend the next year helping on the farm and teaching so we can save money for Georgetown University Law School in Washington, DC, where he has already been accepted.

CHAPTER TWO

The superintendent is friendly and grandfatherly. He remembers my husband and knows the family's predominance in the community. Coming from a family of very successful potato farmers and ranchers, that they are Japanese is offset by their affluence in this small town. There is a high concentration of Native Americans to bolster white egos. Blacks are nonexistent in this Mormon community. We are hired for the year. We present no credentials or certifications other than his degree from Harvard and mine from BU. "It's good enough to have graduated from a four-year college east of the Mississippi," says the superintendent as he introduces us at the opening school meeting.

I teach seventh and eighth grade special education students, self-contained, all "retarded," and many of whom are Native American. They are not allowed to mingle with the "regular students." Mr. Hughes, the principal, is hokey, homespun, overweight, and very much like a plastic toy—so rotund, he would pop back in place if you were to push him. Mr. Lancer is his assistant principal. Corporeal punishment is permissible with a shellacked two-inch thick wooden paddle with holes placed intermittently on its surface. I am asked to witness a paddling in his office. I am enraged at this punitive and primitive measure, but again, my protest is silent. I just leave the room.

DUSTIN AND DESIREE

Dustin and Desiree are Native American twins. They live in a trailer with no doors on the outskirts of town. Like so many of their peers, they are shy and so quiet, yet they are agile and athletic. I am told they cannot take physical education with the other children. They cannot be included in regular middle school classes. We create our own schedule; we create our own community. I enroll them in the "Special Olympics," and we walk to the high school track where we train each day. I time them as they run sprints—the twenty-yard dash, the long jump, and the quarter-mile run around the track. On field day, my students win blue ribbons for every event.

Just before the long Thanksgiving weekend, Dustin and Desiree seem more subdued than normal. They have been enthusiastic about school and come every day. We talk about the plans for the holiday and what traditions are important in their families. Finally, Desi speaks up and says their dog ate the raw turkey that their mother had on the sink counter. I tell them we will get another turkey, but they become very agitated and tell me no. Their mother has told them not to speak about it to anyone; she is very proud. I drive by their trailer at the end of the day. A brown tarp covers the doorway, and the yard is strewn with discarded beer bottles and trash. A thin, wiry, and unfriendly dog sits vigil on the wooden pallet that serves as a step to their home.

As May approaches and students get out of school early to work on the farms, we create our own graduation ceremony for the eighth graders. I bring cake and punch, and we send invitations to parents. My mother-in-law makes graduation certificates and ties them in rolls with red satin ribbon. The students make speeches, and everyone has a part in the ceremony. All I recall about the principal is that he told us not to be seen downtown before 3:00 PM, or "the community might think we don't have enough work to do."

With a summer of my husband moving irrigation pipes or unplugging lines and me housecleaning and cooking on the farm—and the additional pounds put on from eating white sticky rice (prepared literally for every meal)—now coming to an end, we cross the country to Washington, where my husband enrolls in law school. It is late August of 1970, and a year from college graduation, I am again unemployed. We have enough money for the first-semester tuition and a one-bedroom apartment on Rhode Island Avenue in Northwest, DC. A call on an ad for Mason County Public Schools eventually results in a conversation with the assistant principal of Hawthorn High School in Virginia. He says, "We have an opening," and with a snicker, he adds, "depending on how badly you want to teach."

CHAPTER THREE

I am hired after one brief interview to teach in a ninth to twelfth grade self-contained special education program. I am not certified in special education, but that doesn't seem to matter for this position on the eve of opening day. The school is in a rural area, the farthest west end of Mason County, ten miles beyond Tysons Corner, where the Ford dealership is the last sign of retail civilization. The farmland is rolling and lush off Route 7. Reston is still someone's utopian dream, and the culture of megamansions yet to take hold.

I am introduced to the director of special education, Margaret Stewart, a stylish short lady with a husky voice from years of chain-smoking. She meets me at an orientation session and brings me together with my new department chairperson. "This is Iris," Meg says. "She will be heading the new program at the high school." Iris is superorganized and efficient, drives an American-made convertible, and is from "the wrong side of the tracks" in Point Pleasant, New Jersey. Her husband, Al, is studying at the local community college to be an accountant, but they met where she waitressed and he bartended at a beach restaurant in Asbury Park. All this I found out within minutes of meeting her. Meg guides us around tables of new educational materials and equipment. The books, workbooks, controlled readers, overheads, and tape recorders with individual earphones astound me. "Pick out anything you want," Meg barks as she networks her way around the room. Iris is making lists but still revealing her life story to me. "So I say to Al, we need to get an apartment in DC, and I'll teach while you go to school. We plan to have kids and get a nice house. Al's dream was to open his own restaurant, but I told him he was smarter than that and should be an accountant. You and your husband could come to dinner

Saturday night. We live in Arlington. The apartment is small, but we're just like you—you know, starting out. We could plan the new program. It will be with a vocational emphasis. These kids need to be able to work."

The class of EMR students, twenty-six of them, range in reading level from first to eighth grade. It is a newly integrated school, and most of the students are black. Meg is innovative and always telling us to "take the lid off . . . think out of the box." We create a bustling open space with individual learning centers. When students enter the room in the morning, they check a ten-foot bulletin board with all their names going across the top. Under each name are color-coded tags with fifteen—to twenty-minute modules of varying assignments—controlled reader, tape recorder, reading recognition, reading comprehension, vocabulary, math, current events, etc. Their activities change as they move from center to center, and Iris and I are stationed to provide individual and small-group instruction. The planning is grueling. I spend three hours per night and six on weekends deciding which tasks each individual student will do to ensure progress. Their work is assessed daily so all new assignments reinforce what they have learned from the previous day and they are ready to move on. The afternoon session is all vocationally oriented. There is a shampoo bowl and nail station for cosmetology. Harry, a sharply dressed young teacher, takes some of the boys for "custodial careers," and they learn the proper way to mop a floor, mix chemicals, and maintain cleaning equipment. We order appliances for a kitchen space, and students learn to prepare recipes, grocery shop, and observe proper table etiquette. Iris teaches résumé writing and work habits and contacts work sites in the small town for student internships. She is a taskmaster who refuses to allow students to use their disability as an excuse for failure. Strapping adolescents are afraid of incurring her wrath. "You were absent, and you didn't *call!* What do you *think* will *happen* to you if you do that on a real *jooobb!*"

Meg's central office budget provides whatever we need. We have weekly field trips to Washington, and these rural students are in awe of the cafeteria's revolving food wheel at the Smithsonian. They explore the

Capitol, the FBI, the archives, and the treasury. We take them to the new Dulles airport, and they ride the shuttles from the terminal to the plane and interview the driver. They make lists of all the possible jobs at every site visited and write journals back in class about what they have seen and what skills are required for each position. They learn to scour the newspapers; do mock budgets to purchase cars, rent houses, buy groceries; and prepare their own income taxes.

Within three years, we create a program that commands the attention of Eunice Shriver. She visits the class and is visibly impressed with the individualized instruction, the scope of the modular schedule, the use of technology, and the initiative and composure exhibited by the students. This isolated class of students is not part of the Hawthorn High School community, but they seamlessly become part of the competitive workforce of the DC metropolitan area upon graduation. Mrs. Schriver declares it a "model" program.

JAMES

When his father was sent to jail, James went to live with an uncle and aunt and four younger cousins in their apartment in Falls Church and slept on the living room couch. Employed as a custodian at Hawthorn, his uncle obtained special permission for James to attend Hawthorn High School so he could keep an eye on him. Because his uncle had to be at school by 5:30 AM and there was no place for James to wait unsupervised before school opened, I offered to pick him up in the morning. The apartment, reminiscent of army barracks, was on the first floor of a two-story brick building. When I arrived the first time, promptly at 7:00 AM, several of the male residents were sitting on the stoop to escape the sweltering heat that plagued Washington through September. I sat in my Oldsmobile Cutlass, doors locked, having entered a dubious section of the neighborhood. I was met with sullen and suspicious glares until eventually James emerged from the door and picked his way around the tenants with his mug of chocolate milk and got in the car. By the second week, the neighbors were shouting out to him, "C'mon, J! Don't keep your teacher waitin'." As we pulled out of the neighborhood, I had to make a left turn at a busy intersection onto Route 7, and James would look right and say, "You good this side, boss."

Chapter Four

The program grows exponentially, and several more teachers are hired. Iris and her husband move to the Eastern Shore so Al can pursue training with IBM and they can start their family. I am promoted as a specialist for Area 3 special education programs in the county and chair a task force of teachers to develop a K-12 curriculum to be replicated in other schools in the county. I meet regularly with central office personnel who applaud my passion and enthusiasm for this population of students. Meg and I have become dear friends, and I help her by sitting with her aging mother in the later stages of Parkinson's disease while Meg attends meetings.

I am asked to make a presentation to the community, which is held at the General Motors auditorium in Masonville. The place is mobbed, and I confidently talk about this exciting and innovative program, this academic and vocational integration of instruction for students classified as "educable mentally retarded." I am eight and a half months pregnant; law school is over, and my husband has landed a job on Capitol Hill as a senator's administrative aide. We borrow $7,000 from each of our parents and put a down payment on a three-story townhouse in the now burgeoning utopian-style community of Reston.

While on maternity leave with my newborn twins, I return to school to study for a masters in secondary school administration. In a very short career span, I have learned enough to know there are several essential components to good education:

1. Hardworking, gifted teachers

2. Supervisors who nurture, foster autonomy, and presume professionalism
3. Students who are taught from where they are, whatever that place—intellectual, emotional, psychological
4. Learning equates to engagement. One cannot learn uninterested; learning fosters interest, promotes engagement, and inspires participation in the process.
5. One size does not fit all.

Within two years, I am special education certified and graduate with a 4.0 from Virginia Tech with a masters in school administration. I prepare to resume my former position in Mason County, having been interviewed for an assistant principal position at Morris Hall High School and rejected. On my first day back teaching at Hawthorn, I receive a call from the principal of Morris Hall, Mr. Fitch. "They want me to hire a woman," he says (forget the "Hello, how are you?"). "And so, if it has to be a woman, then I'll take you." (Thanks, Gloria Steinhem.)

It is a mega-high school, above 2,500 students. I am one of four assistant principals, assigned a segment of the alphabetical population to mete out discipline. As the newest administrator, I also will cover AM parking lot duty, cafeteria duty, bus duty, drills, and just about every entry-level administrative job imaginable. I approach each task with naive passion. It is a top-performing football school. So when I tire of the game football players play, leaving their trays with half-eaten lunches on cafeteria tables for the custodians to pick up, I go to their coach. The tray game ceases. The custodian, a graying man in his sixties, is a silent and ignored presence as he polishes windows, door frames, and display cases and mops up after affluent, entitled adolescents. I enjoy his company; he is appreciative of my football team intervention, and I am of his work. He seems to accept his "place" in the underbelly of the system. I tell him I am going to Philadelphia to look at the Parkway Program, an alternative school for troubled adolescents. He shares the fact that he owns a street of rundown row houses on the waterfront and I should be sure to try a special restaurant on the block. This silent aging sweeper has the grace and poise of a benign monarch and, probably by now, a matching bank account.

Morris Hall is a high-achieving school with a diverse population, most of whom are college-bound. But I am drawn to the few who cut classes and, I suspect, deal drugs. I sit with binoculars on the second floor of a nearby church that has a clear view of the smoking pit behind the school. Kids pass wrapped packets and exchange money. I take a walk in a nearby park during lunch hour and disperse a group of students at a picnic table who quickly return to campus, leaving me to face two suspicious adults who remain at the table. I report to Mr. Fitch that I think there is a drug issue with some of the students. He dismisses the report, claiming, "The parents wouldn't like that." I offer to contact the superintendent, and he mumbles, "Uh, you could . . ." I place a call to the superintendent's office and identify myself and, surprisingly, am put right through to Harley Traub himself.

With a brief background, I get to the part when I say, "So, Dr. Traub, I believe there is a serious drug problem among some of the students."

He shouts, "THERE IS NO DRUG PROBLEM IN MASON COUNTY SCHOOLS!"

I offer to speak to the Board of Education and report my findings, and exasperated, he says, "NOOOOO! *You* will *not speak* to the board!"

I modulate my tone to a soft, calming pitch, feeling like I am talking my way out of a bomb about to be detonated. Dr. Traub lowers his voice. I tell him I know how much he cares for the students—that has been clear in his message to the staff on opening day. He agrees and says, "Well, I never take off my 'kid' hat since it's all about the kids." I tell him how much I appreciate his time and assure him perhaps I overreacted and didn't mean to disturb him, etc., etc. Within six months, Dr. Traub is appointed the state commissioner of education for the State of Virginia, and Nancy Reagan comes up with the slogan of the decade, Just Say No.

Chapter Five

Over the next two years, with the help of two guidance counselors assigned to my team, I design and implement what is known as the ACT I Program (administrative counseling team year one). We propose to be assigned to the most problematic students who are truant, failing, disengaged, and consume disciplinary time. We provide individual and group counseling sessions for substance abuse and, by the second year, have recruited a team of core academic teachers to provide interdisciplinary instruction for this group of approximately fifty students. It is 1977, and drugs are rampant in public high schools. Nancy Reagan makes reference to ACT I as a model program.

For the next fifteen years, I will take a detour from education. I will lose my land-surveyor father on the eve of his retirement to a blood clot caused by a snapping tree branch. I will separate and divorce my husband of seven years and will earn three times my administrative salary working in the box office at Lincoln Center in New York City. I will meet and marry my husband of now thirty years and give birth to my third child.

The "mommy" years will include the selection of separate private schools for all three of my children and a five-year career owning my preferred theater ticket business and another four years as a megamansion real estate agent in Potomac, Maryland. My mother will tell me she changed my address and phone number nine times over that period. My passion turned to the raising of my own children.

In 1993, while at an appointment for a routine college physical for my daughter, I asked her doctor to check out a lump I had detected in my breast.

I was immediately sent to radiology, had a biopsy within twenty-four hours, and was diagnosed with stage-four breast cancer. Following a mastectomy and the prognosis of "limited time" on this earth, I declined follow-up chemotherapy, and we decided to move our family back to New York from Washington. Once settled in my childhood home in New York, my husband continued with his financial planning business, the older children were ensconced in college, and our youngest entered the sixth grade at Woodstream Elementary School.

CHAPTER SIX

As each anniversary of my surgery passed and my subsequent checkups continued to indicate a pulse, I began to apply for administrative openings in Cornwall County. In New York State, certification rules. Since my license in Virginia bore no weight in New York (forget Eunice and Nancy's endorsement), I began the tedious and cumbersome process of becoming certified. At that time, one could only reach a series of voice mail options to press in the State Education Department, so it literally took close to a year to complete this process. While on hold, I enrolled in SUNY Albany doctoral classes and volunteered as executive director of a student theater group in which my young son had gotten involved. My work consisted of fund-raising, costume storage and cleaning, ticket sales, registration, program graphics and design, providing cases of water and snacks for rehearsals and performances, and hosting monthly board of directors meetings. It was through this connection that my name was mentioned, and out of the blue, really, I received a call from the assistant superintendent of the Woodland Valley Central School district, asking me if I would be interested in an interim principal position at Woodstream Elementary School.

CHAPTER SEVEN

My interview was in January as the position would begin February 1. I drove to my old high school following similar bus routes I had taken as a child. The building looked worn but had a second-floor addition on the west end. The central offices were located in the basement of the building, and I was ushered in by a somewhat familiar face of a woman in her fifties wearing corduroy pants and one of those sweaters with a decorated Christmas tree on it. I later realized she had gone to school with my sister and we had ridden the same bus. A fashion note here—the Washington, DC, area flourished with high-end retailers: Neiman Marcus, Saks Fifth Avenue, Bloomingdales, and best of all possible worlds, Loehmann's. As a realtor in Potomac, my first house commission was spent at Saks in Chevy Chase where a personal shopper brought me a Donna Karan suit with accessories, to which I added shoes on my way out the door. My daily work wardrobe spelled designer, and not only didn't I own a pair of corduroy pants, I also didn't have a single pair of shoes without a minimum three-and-a-half-inch heel. My hair had painted highlights from Frederic Fekkai, and I actually came close to selling a thirty-thousand-square-foot house to a royal family member from the Middle East. But being a homegrown girl from Cornwall County, I was not uncomfortable with the homey atmosphere of this district office and the Mr. Rogers—like demeanor of the superintendent who wore a Mr. Rogers sweater and was just finishing up a bowl of soup when I walked in his door. Dr. Carl Redding greeted me like an old friend. He possessed the understated confidence of a man who you couldn't surprise or impress, and you would only evoke amusement if you tried. He was—and I hope still is—a wise, thoroughly seasoned educator who was all "about the kids." Dr. Carl had come to the Woodland Valley District as a breath of fresh air, a pendulum swing from a regime of authoritarian, rule-from-the-top-down, boss management. The district was still treading lightly around him, unsure that this empowering leader was for real. He met me at Woodstream Elementary on my first day and, with a smile on his face, said, "Good luck."

For eighteen months, I served as interim principal. The favorite slogan of the entrenched staff of teachers seemed to be "In the past, this is how we did it" or "It is dictated by past precedence." Teachers tend to mirror the positional power they adopt with children in the relationship they develop with an administrator. It was amazing to me to see how "personal" the issue of discipline could become. Desk dumping had been a "past precedent." Desk dumping is turning a desk over so its contents spill on the floor, thereby humiliating the offending second grader in front of his or her peers, with the anticipated effect being to correct the infraction of a "disorganized desk." Actually, the "effect" would surface some ten years later in the form of graffiti spray painted on the exterior of a school building—or a desk thrown at a teacher or perhaps even a weapon brought to school, with the intent to do harm.

There is a noticeable disparity between this artistic, laid-back community that is famous for rebelling against the conventional wisdoms of a traditional society and the palpable tenor of the school. Teachers, for the most part, are old school in their philosophy, and the innovative thinking of Kozol, Holt, and Glasser is foreign and intimidating to them. It is a chalk-and-talk school with rows of desks and learning quartered and meted out in scheduled segments around contractual prep periods, duty-free lunches, and required number of professional obligations. The extent to which students are allowed to express themselves is as limited as the number of wrong answers permissible on their worksheets. Staff collaboration on learning projects is nonexistent, although the faculty room is bustling with the latest gossip regarding contract negotiations and parents to "watch out for." There are a few golden teachers who somehow remain immune to the toxic fumes of some of the veteran staff. The librarian, a gifted musician and artist in her own right, welcomes students to the library, where they eagerly share found bugs or spiders from the playground, which leads to an exploration of arachnids and indigenous flora and fauna of the Catskill region. She quietly tells me one evening, as she is leaving late, that the students love me and that I am an inspiration for change, but I should be wary of the "players" who can make life difficult. I encourage her to start a student-conductor program in collaboration with the new music teacher who is teaching students to compose music.

I bring in a modern-dance instructor who captivates students over a three-day workshop on movement and attention, which culminates in a final performance that delights and overwhelms parents and evokes complaints from the "players" that "too much instructional time has been wasted." Students approach me with the idea to have a student council, and I tell them to find a teacher who they would like to have as an adviser. They canvass the school and return with no recruits, so I set up the student government myself; we hold elections and meet during lunch periods in a vacant classroom.

The cafeteria during lunch is a chaotic period supervised by classroom aides who raise their hands when the noise level gets too high. This is the first venting session students have from self-contained classroom instruction with their assigned grade teacher. I propose that we start a "reservation table" and tell students they can sign up to be at the table and are allowed to invite one guest. The new reservation table is set up on the stage of the cafetorium, and I bring in a freshly laundered white tablecloth with a bunch of yellow tulips. The selected students for the week invite their guests, some of whom are parents and some teachers. Lunch is brought up from the regular cafeteria. For the weeks the reservation table is in operation, not once is there a spill or smudge from food. Students take ownership of the table and converse with their peers and their guests with enthusiasm and poise. I am soon approached by the union rep one afternoon, who requests that I announce to students that they no longer can invite their teachers as a guest at the reservation table. The rationale, I am told, is that teachers "deserve a break" without their students, and it is best if the "new rule" comes from the administrator so they (the teachers) didn't look like "the bad guys."

My faculty meetings are theme oriented. I share articles about up-and-coming educational programs and gently introduce the concept of teaming and collaboration as an instructional strategy for the new year. I develop a master schedule enabling teachers to meet during common team planning periods, and I relieve them of playground supervision (the carrot that enables them to at least attempt to explore this change). Word is spreading in the community that the new interim principal is "great," and parents tell me they support the new initiatives. One morning, I am invited to a parent coffee at one of the family homes. We sit in a circle on a conglomeration of chairs, a couch, and some sit on the floor, balancing coffee cups and Danish. The spokesparent begins by telling me how happy they are with the new look of Woodstream and that they are hopeful for the first time about their children's schooling. I notice these are parents who attend PTA meetings but rarely speak. The PTA vocals are aligned with many of the teachers. When I return to school, I am met by the rep who accuses me of attending a "secret" meeting of parents behind their backs. I feel as though I am in a bad espionage movie. Did I actually break a rule going to a parent's home for a meeting? Who even knew I was at the meeting? Did one of the parents get on the phone and call the rep while I was backing out of the driveway? I didn't go to discredit the teachers or the school for that matter, but to listen to their concerns and get to know them. I encourage the "secret meeting" parents to attend the next PTA and voice their concerns, and I will be there to facilitate an honest exchange. Their response is "to leave it alone" since they do not want any repercussions on their children.

The teacher "players" amount to about three people and, not surprisingly, include the rep woman. After eighteen months, the interim position becomes available as a full-time permanent position, so of course, I apply. The job is "posted," and like all school positions, a "shared decision making" team is recruited. These hiring teams, depending on the position, are comprised of "stakeholders" that include teachers, nonteaching personnel (clerical, custodial), an administrator, and a parent. The team meets to determine what questions will be asked, and according to very "strict" guidelines, the same questions are asked of each candidate. All of the preparations are kept highly confidential, including the names and histories of the candidates until the big interview day. Since I am the sitting principal in the school, I only have to travel down the hall from my office to the faculty room when my designated time slot comes up. I am feeling pretty good about the process. Sure, there have been disagreements, but I have gently moved Woodstream from a closed to a more open community school. The curriculum has been enriched by taking advantage of the local artist resources. Inroads have been made in the way in which the curriculum is delivered, and students are happy and eager to come to school. The finale event, the sixth grade graduation, was testimony to how well the once-divisive forces united in a positive way for the good of the students.

When my son was a sixth grade graduate from the same school, I remember, following the ceremony, groups of students and parents dispersed to private parties and family events. One student, whom my son had befriended, was left standing alone with his single-parent mom as other students received gifts and headed off to special events. I decided if there was to be celebration, all students should be able to participate and not be excluded since they had not made the right invitation list. For this graduation, I proposed a school-wide event to the PTA. Within a very short time, a father who was a DJ on the side offered his services; parents who owned a restaurant offered to cook; drinks, paper goods, and even a graduation cake were volunteered. I rented a tent and dance floor to hedge against rain (which we had), and the rest is the history of a memorable event that left students exhilarated and parents in tears of gratitude. Even the rep was seen dancing in her one-size-fits-all muumuu.

When I entered the faculty room for my interview, there they were, the three "players" and the PTA vocals. I was summarily rejected. I had the pleasure of taking the new principal for a tour around the building I had come to view as my own a few days later. I wished him good luck. Within a year, he had been terminated. It is an old joke among superintendents—"I believe in shared decision making: I make the decision, then share it with others." Why doesn't this process sound logical to me? Is it sour grapes on my part, perhaps, having been rejected time and time again, only to find the position was not a "legitimate" opening but "posted," which is required by law, but then the preferred candidate was manipulated into place?

There are the stakeholders—holders of interest in the school, students, and/or community. It would seem one could have a few teachers, an administrator, a classroom aide, a secretary or custodian, and a student, and collectively they could determine the best candidate for a given position. However, the goal isn't necessarily to select the best candidate; rather, it is the person the team can agree upon to "live with." Rarely does a team unanimously agree upon a candidate. That they can live with that person is a concession—to settle for, to tolerate. Then there is the reference check. There is the phone interview as the reference checker goes down the form: Do you work collaboratively? What are your strengths and weaknesses? Would you reemploy? What is your overall rating?

Where does the training in human resources factor in? We all react to people in different ways, but the first reaction is emotional: How do they look? What is the demeanor, voice pitch, body language? From that less than accurate assessment, the team will judge, question by question, according to what nerve the candidate has hit: too talented, too smart, too pretty, too prejudiced, self-absorbed, overconfident, too immature, too young, too old, too fat, too thin, too high style, too sloppy, too friendly, too stiff. Nonetheless, better than one person making the decision—one opinion, one judgment. At least, as a team, no one person can be blamed; and at least, as a team, we can agree on the level to which the bar cannot go lower—that level of person we all can "live with."

CHAPTER EIGHT

Over the course of my administrative career, I have attended hundreds of meetings—faculty, departmental, cross curricular, health and safety, administrative council/cabinet, budget, case management, leadership team, committee on special education, superintendent hearings, conferences, parent-teacher, mentor, and on and on. The content of any of these meetings, which lasted a minimum of one hour to a marathon six hours, could be condensed to ten minutes, perhaps less.

Easily, the first twenty minutes is consumed with "cover up" activities—superficial jokes and greetings, pad-pencil organization, food distribution, message checking, last-call restroom visits (although sometimes, the exits occur further into more sensitive parts of the discussion), icebreaker activities (my all-time least favorite), and overall territorizing of individual chair and table space. Sometimes there is an agenda, usually a list of one-word bulleted items, such as "icebreaker" to "questions" or "other" at the bottom of the list. This vague and useless guideline gives the group time to silently gauge the level at which they may or may not participate and the chances that they may be called upon to report out. There is always a "fluffer" who will posture for "good girl, good boy" attention, who will bring up some off-topic item—"good food drive effort" or "great basketball game the other night."There is an appointed leader—superintendent, assistant superintendent, principal, department chairperson, whoever. Sometimes, their own personal and professional discomfort in this revered position keeps them perseverating on off-color jokes or self-deprecating stories about the money spent on a bad vacation or a problem with the Mercedes.

The meeting participants keep it going, and the hour erodes closer and closer to lunch or buses. If the meeting is after school—and you better watch this one—the absolute maximum cutoff is between 3:30 and 4:00 PM, 3:30 PM FOR SURE IF IT IS A FACULTY MEETINg. The day of the week matters: Wednesdays are reserved for union business; Tuesdays and Thursdays are great for doctor's appointments; Mondays are good faculty meeting days; and Fridays are 100 percent totally and categorically off-limits. Just prior to the magic 3:30 or 4:00 PM limit, the meeting-ites will begin a somewhat noticeable shuffling of papers, checking of watches, putting of caps back on pens, and repositioning of coats, umbrellas, and briefcases. As others join in the dance of the meeting closing activities, moods alter. Anticipation and enthusiasm diminish. Cynicism returns. They are already preparing for the grocery stop, child-care pickup, dentist appointment, highway battle, or in some cases, the trek back to their own office to sift through phone messages and e-mails. The "real meeting" assessment begins: "Well, that was a waste," "He's sooo out of touch . . . can't make a decision . . . full of himself." But for that day, we have covered the necessary ground. We have been in a meeting, and with that singularly powerful, simple word to conjure up our inflated importance ("Sorry, I've been in a meeting"; "I've had nothing but meetings all day long!"; "One meeting after another . . ."), we justify our highly compensated time.

Calculate just the average salary of a district's administrators for an hour. What have they generated in revenue sitting around the table? Into what educational benefit will it translate? What student's life will be changed? What good comes out of it? What an excuse for the justification of what you cannot accomplish. "I was in a meeeeeting" and the paycheck will be there, without conditions or delay, on payday.

CHAPTER NINE

Dr. Carl calls my home around 5:30 PM and says, "Good evening, Dr. R. [He always calls me doctor even though he knows I have not completed the degree.] I have some news for you, but you cannot tell a soul yet."

I had just completed my interview for the high school principal position at Woodland Valley High, which was posted shortly after the elementary position was filled with my competition. "Yes, Dr. Carl?"

"The committee has selected you as the new principal of the high school."

"Reeeaaally?" I squeal.

It is early June, and I will officially begin the position on July 1. My dream of becoming a high school principal has come true.

I arrive early, just before bus dismissal. I am going to be introduced to the faculty as the new principal. I was waiting in my car in the parking lot when a container of yogurt is thrown from a second-floor window and splatters on the blacktop. It is the last day of school and just prior to bus dismissal. As I enter the building, the middle school principal and the high school assistant principal are chasing students who are throwing water balloons. Their hand radios crackle, "I need men! All custodial staff on the main floor!" Water sloshes with litter from a locker cleanout in the hallways, making a slippery mess to navigate to the meeting in the cafeteria. Teachers sit at round tables drawn and weary, and there is a sense of dread and skeptical expectancy as I enter the room. Dr. Carl is assisted by the interim principal and the assistant principal to quiet the conversations among some 170 teachers and staff. I thank them profusely for the privilege of being their next principal. My smile is genuine and my voice enthusiastic, both of which seem out of place given the harrowing day they must have just experienced. It is over within minutes. The interim informs me he will be staying on another three weeks to assist with the transition, but he has packed his office so I can move in, and he will be in a smaller adjoining space. I tell Dr. Carl I really would prefer starting right out on my own and that a three-week transition is unnecessary. The interim comes to me the next day and tells me he "has a deal to stay three more weeks, and he is staying." Two and a half of those weeks he spent packing up the Regents exams (that task, at most, would take a few hours). He took my (formerly his) secretary to lunch, and I gave up deleting his juicy e-mails to a "friend" from another district, including an itinerary of secret liaisons, and had to ask the tech person for assistance to decontaminate my computer. (Going rate for an interim administrator in the area—around $550 a day.)

I set about doing what I can do under the watchful eye of Mr. Scandel, who busily reports my every move to the assistant principal and the residing-under-the-same-roof middle school principal. I declutter my office, set up my files, and buy new burgundy leather furniture at John's Used Office Furniture and a set of beautiful forest-green drapes from Pottery Barn. The AP (who kept the biggest office, with the early American decor and the plastic eagles on the pressboard bookcase) tells me my office reminds him of his brother's funeral parlor. In exploring all the spaces with my grandmaster key, I come upon a huge walk-in storage closet, dusty and moldy and filled with mice droppings and mildew that probably dates back to my kindergarten days. There are old files, discipline reports of students from the 1950s, and attendance cards and course scheduling cards from the days of data entry clerks. There are damp, disintegrating books, unopened faded packages of construction paper in every color of the rainbow, and cases of yellow chalk. There are broken tape recorders, overhead projectors, and various missing parts to equipment not identified. I am struck by the enormous waste of materials, the paper documents, some of which are worthy of archiving, and the disheartening lack of organization. I ask one of the custodians to bring me some trash bags, and I begin salvaging materials and trashing others as I inch myself into the room. I am wearing a white linen pencil skirt with a sleeveless black top and black high heels. I ditch the heels to stand barefoot on a chair to reach the shelves of broken bookcases. Above me, on open rafters that lead to the projection booth over the auditorium, there are more boxes—semicrushed and stuffed. I find cigarette butts and think what a firetrap this has been.

The AP strolls by (twelve-month contract for administrators) on his way to "the dentist" and says, "So you found the place where the kids go to have sex, huh?" with his typically sarcastic smirk.

"Yes, just trying to give them a little more space to maneuver in here."

Jake, the head custodian, gets word of what I am doing, and several clerical staff from guidance report that the new principal is "in her bare feet." Jake sends Bobbie up with a Dumpster on wheels as I am slowly but surely filling the main hall with debris, and the "trash bags just aren't gonna hold up, Ms. R." It is the middle of summer, and the skeletal staff is witnessing firsthand a physical reorganization and cleansing that is also silently conveying the message that we will reopen in September with a new look. The school is filthy and neglected. Lightbulbs are burned out; the brass handrails going up the staircases are tarnished black. Glass display cases have broken shelves and are filled with dead flies and cobwebs. "Think of it as a beautiful hotel lobby with glistening floors," I cheerily say as the passersby gaze wide-eyed and dumbfounded. The secretaries jump on board and begin sifting through files piled high on the main office countertops. Ana makes new curtains, and Ellen brings in lush-green hanging plants.

Jake's guys assume a new level of energy in their custodial summer work. I ask Dr. Carl for one major expenditure, justifying it by saying, "The school needs to feel more welcoming. Students need to know we respect them enough to provide a clean and organized environment, so pul-leeeeze, I *have* to have the halls and the lockers painted." The old dull-blue lockers darken the corridors, and the blue paint is scraped and filled with graffiti. The walls are dull beige with green tiles that start halfway down the wall and go to the floor. Dr. Carl approves the paint, and soon the white upper walls and the seafoam-green tiles blend with the shiny lockers to create a muted soft color to the corridors.

Teachers come in, dressed in the unmistakable fashion of backyard summer, to check on the readiness of their classrooms. My office door opens to the main hall, so when they glance in, I beckon them to come in. We chat easily about their vacation, and I make a conscious attempt to avoid talk about work and the new year. "How wonderful you went to Europe" or "Congratulations on the new baby" and "Enjoy the rest of your summer!" A veteran and outspoken (very unhappy) foreign language teacher brazenly skips the introductions and says to me, "What's this I hear about a hotel lobby? We can't have kids hanging out in the halls!" By Labor Day, we are ready to open. Large pots filled with red geraniums and ivy rest on either side of the main entrance. The school is beautiful; the terrazzo is restored to its original shine, and the brass rails glisten. I tell Jake to order lunch for the crew as my treat. Jake sets up sawhorses in the garage bay near the loading dock and invites the custodians from all the other schools in the district to a big Chinese luncheon. One and all they timidly make their way to thank me. "Oh nooo, thank *yoouuuu*!" I tell them that without their work, there would be no educational program, that they create the environment for learning; they create the aura for mutual respect. And this is true. Administrators beware—your right-hand guy is the custodian, and the right-hand girl is the nurse!

When students arrive, I am in the crowded halls, smiling, greeting them with "good morning" and "welcome back" (and I will learn every name of the 1,200 students). They may or may not know who I am, but I have master keys jangling from a bracelet and a walkie-talkie. Some return my smile, and some pretend not to be curious; others are too absorbed in greeting their friends from a summer's absence. At 9:00 AM, I schedule a school-wide assembly. "Not a good idea," the middle school principal says, and my AP concurs, "Could be disruptive, give them a couple days to settle down." But the announcement is made, and teachers come with their classes, crowding down the auditorium aisles and filling every seat. I see Dr. Carl come in and stand along the wall in the very back. I have already asked the custodians to come and sit down in the orchestra pit facing the audience where the microphone is placed. As I approach the mic, the chatter and laughter and adolescent hoots silence. (I know I have about thirty seconds to keep this crowd or lose them.) I introduce myself as their new principal and invite them to join me in thanking the custodial staff for preparing a beautiful school for their return. I motion the custodians to stand, and they are greeted with resounding applause and cheers. They seem embarrassed yet proud at this overwhelming display of attention. They bask in that beautiful moment and then walk up the steps to resume their day. I do not remember exactly what I said—only that I had rehearsed a sequence of things I wanted to share about what a school should mean to them. They listened with rapt attention, and I was, at a higher conscious level, aware of myself actually capturing their attention. Like a plunge from a high diving board, a skid on ice going down a hill, walking a tight rope, or an event where you just function on instinct—where you cannot retreat or stop or start over or walk away, but you have to keep going—I spoke of their need to participate in their education, to plan and propose and create and craft their programs, to have dreams and figure out ways to use school and its resources to realize them. I spoke about the first lines in the Harry Potter series, written on a table napkin by a penniless single mother. I spoke about Bill Gates who dropped out of Harvard but created Microsoft. No more than ten or fifteen minutes later, I ended with, "Good luck to you all!" The applause was instantaneous, and I was grateful it was long and enthusiastic. "They liked me," as Sally Fields once said when she received her Academy Award.

There was one student in the second row to my immediate left who occasionally made a comment to his adjacent friend and laughed. Although it was not a discernible disruption to anyone short of me and those few immediately around him, I memorized his face and made a point to catch up with him later in the day. During the lunch period, I scoured the cafeteria and the outside patio. I saw him stretched out on a slope of grass, holding court with three or four friends. I walked across the patio and up the grassy slope in my three-inch heels, fully aware of my audience from the lunch crowd. He looked at me, and I said hi and asked him his name.

He replied, "Why?"

I said, "I figured you wanted to talk since you had so much to say this morning. Is now a good time?"

He was a bright, disenfranchised, bored, artistically talented sophomore. Three years later, I wrote him a recommendation to Bard College, where he was accepted with a lush and extraordinarily beautiful photography portfolio.

The first faculty meeting was similar to the assembly only for the adults, and at least, at a "honeymoon" meeting, there are no interruptions. Always be aware of your audience. Their eyes and posture speak volumes, and be prepared to hold them by adapting your tone, your physical positioning, and your message delivery. Read them; it is not difficult, but it requires two levels of attention from you: (1) your here and now and (2) your outer view, which is a separate lens with you and them in the picture. Most speakers stay in their here and now. It is all about them, but effective speaking is all about keeping a constant hand on the pulse of your audience.

STEPHEN

Mr. Brody tells me he is having a real problem with his advanced placement biology class: students are rude and disruptive, don't complete their work, and overall "think the whole class is a joke." He wants me to speak with them and "set them straight." I tell him I will stop in unannounced and at least try to get a sense of what is going on. Mr. Brody is not a rocket-science teacher; he hails from Brooklyn and comes thick with the accent of the city. He is also very ADHD and probably makes the equivalent of his teaching income earning stipends as the adviser for every student club. He is a track coach, student council advisor, sponsor of all student dances, collector of tickets at football games and basketball games (home and away), organizer of the homecoming parade and election of king and queen, and a genuine and passionate believer in students and will do everything in his power to keep them involved in productive and fun activities. I enter his room after class has already begun and take a desk toward the back where I have a full view of the students. Brody doesn't skip a beat and continues the lesson from the smart board but moves abruptly from the board to the right side of the class. He makes eye contact with those students; he asks those students questions and pretty much ignores the students on the left side of the room. In the front row, on the left side of the room, sits Stephen. I notice that whenever Brody turns away from the students and moves toward the board, Stephen leans over and makes a comment. Students to the right of Stephen and those just behind him can hear what he says. There are occasional giggles and smothered chortles, and this continues for some time. Brody gets in the act only to see the after-Stephen reaction but does not know it is Stephen causing the situation. I leave the room and speak with Brody later.

He asks, "What do you think?"

To which, I reply, "Stephen is teaching the class."

"What?"

"Brody, Stephen is teaching the class, so let him teach it. He can do a better job, he knows this stuff inside and out, and you cannot compete with him. Let him plan the lessons and teach the class." (The disruptions were caused as Stephen "corrected" Mr. Brody's frequent misinformation and erroneous conclusions on the subject matter.)

Stephen is a savant. When he exited the SAT exams one Saturday afternoon, his mother asked him how they were. "Cake" was his reply (later confirmed by his perfect score). Stephen went on to be the valedictorian, where he juggled balls while delivering a riveting speech. He was given full scholarships to Harvard, MIT, Stanford, Princeton, and Yale. He chose MIT, where he graduated top of his class, was courted once again by Stanford on full scholarship for a PhD, and will—if he isn't yet—become the most respected leader in genetic research.

Chapter Ten

For five years, the high school flourished, rapidly moving to the top school in the county in enrollment, test scores (Regents, SATs), outstanding performance in national math and science competitions, and number of students college-bound—many of whom attended Ivy League institutions. Special programs involving the cultural arts, field trips to the Metropolitan Opera full-dress rehearsals, museums, art galleries, and the annual trip to Boston for the Harvard Model Congress (we were one of the few public schools accepted to participate) were all part of my budget allocations. Departments congealed, led by extraordinary master teachers in each core subject area and developed advanced placement courses in English, math, science, foreign language, and government. Students created a forum for presidential debates during the national elections, and an astounding, impassioned series of debates over entering the war in Iraq were presented at a school-wide assembly. A very special friend and philanthropist was the catalyst for bringing a film/media elective to our curriculum that was so popular, it evolved (over a three-year period) into three separate programs:

1. Media elective
2. Medialert—an interdisciplinary English-social studies course
3. A community school for especially problematic students

The cost savings to taxpayers providing in-house services—especially for problem students (violence; substance abuse; special psychiatric, emotional, and academic needs)—per pupil, rather than the twenty-five-thousand-dollar tuition paid for the county agency's cooperative services, was mind-boggling. Hundreds of students were served on campus over the course of this four-year period at a fraction of the cost. Dances, proms, college fairs, assemblies, concerts, musicals, athletic competitions, clubs (including "hangouts" for those who had nothing to do in their rural communities after school) abounded and continued without incident. There was no violence, no graffiti, and no teen suicides.

In the fall of 2005, Dr. Carl, going on his eleventh year as superintendent, announced his retirement. "Before we hire a search firm," he opened at the administrative council meeting, "do any of you want it?" In retrospect, I should have raised my hand heartily. But the high school was on a roll; plans were in the works to expand the hugely successful Medialert Program, and we were beginning plans for technology upgrading, and the ever-growing program for high-functioning autistic students had attracted national attention. The superintendent's role seemed so far above and beyond my skill set. Budget planning, board meetings, transportation and personnel and state regulations and compliance issues, hearings and lawsuits, and union negotiations seemed like daunting responsibilities, and Dr. Carl seemed to take them all in stride effortlessly. Yet I had spent the past four years as up close and personal with those issues as anyone as the high school principal. I was a native-born member of the community and had achieved celebrity status at the local markets. I could not buy a box of cereal or a can of cat food without a parent coming up to me and having a fifteen- or twenty-minute discussion. I loved my work, and although I knew I would greatly miss my leader and mentor, I was secure in my commitment to secondary school reformation and was just as confident that I would not stand a chance at moving to a position as esteemed as the superintendency.

The candidate pool was shallow. Two women emerged: one who was serving as an assistant superintendent of a district smaller than the population of my high school, and the other who was an elementary principal in an adjoining district. The shared decision-making team selected the elementary principal, who abruptly withdrew her application upon being appointed superintendent in her own district, and so began the untimely reign of

Gertie. At first glance, she was a warm and friendly grandmotherly type. She was a cancer survivor, wore pants, suits, and blocky rubber-sole shoes. She instituted "snacks" at administrative council, soon to be renamed administrative cabinet, where she invited Jake from custodial, Otto from buildings and grounds, and Jerry from transportation. She had a rotating calendar of duties for these weekly meetings, the most important of which was the administrator assigned to bring the snacks. Gertie brought in her own assistant superintendent (a former secretary who had gone on to get the streamlined crash course version of administrative certifications) and Linda, her own business manager—a young twenty-something with a deer-in-headlights look on her face all the time and naturally curly hair clipped up in a barrette—who had yet to pass her accounting exam and had no administrative or central office experience. Gertie was personable, approachable, and enjoyed a six-month honeymoon as superintendent. As the tough issues began to surface—budget, redistricting, and school closings—she floundered, leaning heavily on meetings with her cabinet for decision making. She ate all the wrong foods for a normal person, let alone one who was a cancer survivor—cheese, creamy dips, doughnuts, cake, and candy. Meetings lasted into lunch, and she would have Gladys, her secretary, take orders for banquet-sized Chinese, pizza, or greasy subs. She prefaced her decisions or recommended positions at board meetings as having been determined by the administrators when, in fact, we had become more factionalized. As her weight ballooned as did the size of her pantsuits, Gertie became suspicious of her assistant superintendent, accusing her of "manipulating" applications for a teaching position that included a relative. The friendly smile gave way to a flushed complexion and a paranoid demeanor. She required all her administrators to be present at board meetings to show solidarity and assigned each of us a turn at being a facilitator of the cabinet meetings. During one anticipated, particularly contentious meeting in early January, Linda decorated the conference room with colored crepe paper streamers and confetti, passed out noisemakers and party hats, and made a huge sheet cake with "Happy New Year" written over the top of the thick white frosting. During a heated discussion of programs to be saved or eliminated, confetti stuck to administrator's clothing as the streamers sagged above us over the conference table. My new AP, a thirty-five-year-old former teacher, would occasionally blow on his party horn when the tension became too thick.

Gertie lasted eighteen months before succumbing to a reoccurrence of cancer. While still at the helm and shakily walking with a cane as her weight dramatically shrank, she orchestrated the "successor" process. She recruited the father of her young business manager as an interim to ease the transition and navigate the search. Her sole most important criterion for her successor was that they be a "sitting superintendent." That alone excluded any possible candidates from her own cabinet. Gertie never forgot the tense and confrontational meeting dynamics, or perhaps she was just angry at her own untimely demise. During her last few months, the interim (an extra $550 per day in his pocket) visits each administrator to glean gossip about the others, which he promptly reports back to Gertie. He is a cagey sort, ingratiating himself with the board members, sufficiently self-deprecating to allow them to think he has no personal agenda; he's just here to help out a friend and do the best by the district. He is also clearly listening to his daughter and has been given the scoop on all of us cabinet members. Linda is clearly interested in keeping her job and has no doubt shared her concern if one of the sitting cabinet members emerged. Assistant superintendent is crossed off the list; Gertie has raised enough suspicion about her sneaking her relative's résumé into the pile to relegate her to the "no" pile. Interim sets the stage with the board, and soon a former superintendent (now unemployed) from another district comes on board as the "real" interim. His reputation as a ladies' man precedes him, and rumors abound that he houses a mistress locally, but the wife, to whom he is still married, lives in New Jersey, and he commutes there on weekends.

At Gertie's funeral, I walk down the side aisle of the church and slide into a pew and find myself seated right next to him and the girlfriend. (I know she is the girlfriend as she is half his age and they are holding hands.) I am immediately feeling nauseated and claustrophobic from the strong odor of his cologne mixing with her perfume. He assumes the position, always starting with the round of individual meetings with administrators so he can get a "read" on the district schools. Then there are more rounds of getting-to-know-yous with board members and parents. Before he has even completed his rounds, we come in one day to find him just gone. A scandal brewing from his former district has finally caught up, and he is just gone, and the superintendent's office is vacant again.

We have final interim success with good ole boy Dave. Passed over for a regional superintendent position a few years earlier, Dave has been in semiretirement. During the winter, he is an instructor at the local rifle range. He is the husband of a teacher in a neighboring district and, with that inside track, understands the "players" from her perspective. Dave begins his first administrative cabinet meeting with a series of jokes (he reads) about his ex-wife. Met with the overly enthusiastic laughter of administrators now on their third interim "leader," Dave tests out a few more "colorful" jokes regarding ethnicity, sexual orientation, and religion. Met with less enthusiasm, he begins the meeting by telling us he's just a "regular guy." He was the handsome charmer whom we could find, between noon and one o'clock, cloistered in the conference room every day holding court with all the central office secretaries who giggled for an hour over their home-brought sandwiches and salads. He was all status quo and streamlined; no significant changes were made, and he produced nothing for his $625 per diem. Since Dr. Carl, we are on the third superintendent in less than a year. Each one started with his eduspeak sales pitch, and each brought to the table his own quirks for either addressing or dismissing issues. As principals, we pretty much ran our own buildings without too much central office oversight. With a significant change in board members, the search for the "real" superintendent is now the task of a one-person search firm for the price of twenty-five thousand dollars. He provides a colorful brochure, setting the stage in the "scenic Catskills," detailing a laundry list of lofty characteristics for the lucky candidate who will have time enough on his or her hands to take advantage of the area's "fishing, boating, skiing, and hiking."

This time, there are three in-house candidates: the middle school principal, Gertie's assistant superintendent, and me. All three of us are scheduled for interviews with the search firm head at a diner "around the corner from [his] office" in Putnam County. My interview lasts over an hour and a half. Ten minutes into the interview, his businesslike and official tone change. He puts down his pen and pushes aside his notepad and just listens. His question had been "What is your take on where the district is and where it should be going?" I detailed the history of the district and where it had been when I was hired, what it had become on the accent, and what was required to restore momentum. I outlined a strategic plan for recovery and cited my knowledge of the administrative "players." I understood the internal operations and behind-the-scene sabotage; I understood how the unions worked and what the board needed in leadership from a superintendent. When we concluded the interview, he walked me across the parking lot to my car and said, "Well, are you ready?" I drove home confident that I had bagged the elephant (old box office term).

After weeks of delay and no news, two candidates were announced and brought before the administrative cabinet for the first of a series of interviews. Both men were from small rural districts north of Albany. When I met them, they were as equally unlikely a match for the district as they were different. One was a manager who offered structure and would "tow the line." The other was a nice guy, unused to pressure and caved within an hour of pummeling questions. (He promptly withdrew his application.) Both had been sitting superintendents. Mr. Search Firm dug back into his file of original applicant rejects and emerged with a third applicant from a rural school in Oregon. Her résumé was at least four or five pages, three of which listed all the books she had ever read. She had held multiple positions—music teacher, substitute, counselor, transportation director, consultant, and a combined position of principal/superintendent. Her degree was from an obscure "university" where she obtained her "doctorate in education," which we later discovered was an isolated building on the side of a busy Oregon highway, known as an online-degree factory. There were huge gaps in her résumé where years were unaccounted for. As a cabinet, we were astounded at the holes and inconsistencies of her portfolio. She flew out to the East Coast three times for each of her interviews but, on the third and final visit, was able to negotiate the airline ticket out of the board. She entered her interview with the administrators and had the look of one highly medicated. Her beady eyes, behind clear framed glasses, darted from one side of the table to the other, in almost a frantic attempt to size up her allies and enemies. Her short obviously colored blond hair was tightly curled in a 1950s beauty parlor style, and she wore a shapeless black skirt with a turquoise jacket with brass buttons, accessorized with black stacked-heel shoes. She alternated her speech between rapid and garbled in a high pitch (more phrenic when she appeared uneasy) and a lower, slower pitch and pace when she wanted to emphasize a point or command attention. When she left the interview, all of us had to fill out evaluation sheets as we had on all previous candidates. Assistant Superintendent didn't hesitate to tear her apart on the sheet, criticizing her every move and pointing out all the inconsistencies in her résumé. The others followed suit and included comments such as "What a joke" and "She can't be serious." I did not complete my evaluation at all. It was beyond comprehension that this person had even gotten this far in the process and, I was sure, would never make it through the final series with board members, teachers, and students. When Gladys, the board clerk and also the secretary to the superintendent, entered the room to collect the evaluations, I slipped my blank sheet in with the completed sheets and, under her hawklike eye, was permitted to leave the room. Later we discovered Mr. Search Firm had dismissed her on the basis of her résumé. Any discerning educator would have. He brought her back to the surface when the board rejected the other candidates (and for some reason, was stuck on the "sitting superintendent" criteria established by Gertie), thinking perhaps they would see the absurdity of her candidacy and perhaps reconsider an in-house administrator. But the board, short one vote, selected Laura Christler and told us to "give her a chance . . . She's lovely." So began the reign of terror by one known among us in the "real" meetings (after the superintendent meetings) as "that crazy lady." Laura began in February and developed a close alliance with Gladys, who provided her with all personnel files to review, along with copies of the feedback evaluations from her own interview. (A note here that part of the protocols of shared decision making call for the shredding of all documents, scrap paper, and notes from the interview process).

Without fail, every day between 3:00 and 3:30 PM, Laura called my office and said, "Please come down now." I would run down the stairs, and she would engage in one inane discussion after another about the rationale for procedures, which either were in place or were not in place, and "What do you know about that?" She called at least half a dozen times during the day and sometimes would have Gladys call for her. "Barbara, some neighbors complained that students are smoking off school property, and the superintendent says 'you need to *do* something about it.'" Other times, Laura would direct that I provide a written summary or historical outline of a program along with a justification for why it was needed. I felt as though I was doing her work—at the very least, providing the training. Then there were times when my answer to Laura's call would be met with the subdued, quiet Laura. "Barbara, I love your shoes. I could never wear shoes like that, but they are soooo lovely. We should go out for a glass of wine sometime." Laura was also bent on going after the administrators who wrote their impressions of her on their interview evaluation forms. Some were bold enough to sign their names. She would attack them out of the blue at cabinet meetings, dismiss their comments, and slowly bury them with useless paperwork. I was tiring of teaching superintendents and paying deference to their personal quirks. I had a school to run and students and staff who needed my attention. She began the committee-meeting phase—break up into groups, do an assigned task, reconvene in the large group, and list the findings from your group with large colored magic markers on chart paper taped around the room. Sometimes she would do this exercise with just the administrative cabinet; sometimes with the teachers. (Gertie's "snack" agendas seemed more productive.) Our ranks divided. The middle school principal announced her retirement; the assistant superintendent would transfer within the year; the director of Pupil Personnel Services would resign within the year; and Rhoda Shackman, one of the elementary principals, would announce her new position as assistant superintendent of the Cornwall County Institute (this arranged marriage had been in the works for some time). When it was announced that Rhoda was leaving, I met with Laura and requested that I be transferred to that elementary school. For a senior tenured administrator with experience as a principal at the elementary level, this was a no-brainer. I should have been granted the transfer. Laura seemed miffed at the request and said she would "think about it." Within two days, she summoned me to her office and said in her high-pitched, singsong voice, "Barbara, I have moved all the chairs around in the dollhouse back and forth, around and around, and I just cannot move you to the elementary school. You need to stay at the high school, there is just no one else who can sit in that chair." I stare at her as she stares at the table and have a vision of her sitting on the floor someplace in her house at night with miniature dollhouse furniture—miniature dolls to represent each one of the principals, sitting in miniature chairs, and her moving them from one to the other, singing.

I could no longer protect the staff or students from the swath of her damage. She was so blinded by her position, perhaps her own disbelief of actually having snowed the district into hiring her after having been driven out of the state of Oregon, that she was obsessed with asserting herself as a woman of power. She committed random acts of abuse of her office. There was no plan or thought or reflection. She created situations where one would appear to be given a choice, only to be set up for blame. Heads were twisted by the chaotic swings of her moods on which she made reckless decisions and demands. The staff was looking to me for some semblance of calm and order, and I was as much being sucked into the vortex of her insanity as anyone else.

I was earning $120,000 a year, more money than I had ever made in my life. I worked conservatively fifty-five hours per week, fifty weeks per year. Never did I take a lunch half-hour, and this did not include hours spent at evening board meetings, dances, concerts, athletic competitions, evening activities, and the months and weeks of preparation for graduation. I was second to Jake on the list to be called in the middle of the night if an alarm went off and, on several occasions, drove out to the building to shine a flashlight through each and every window. This roughly forty-dollars-per-hour pretax salary did include some life insurance and 80 percent health benefits, including eye care, dental, and pension contributions. I had also received tenure, guaranteeing my employment barring a rape, murder, or gross negligence on my part, which would affect the health and safety of my staff and students. From this salary, I also paid for field trips for indigent students; had a running tab at the cafeteria for students without lunch money but who did not qualify for free lunch; supplemented the cost of advanced placement exams for students who could not afford the eighty-dollar fee; paid for students to take the driver education course offered at cost, but unaffordable for many; paid for decorations for holidays, furniture for my own office, as well as coffee and cookies for faculty meetings and parents' back-to-school night. I am not complaining. I was better off than many; I had a successful working husband who paid the mortgage.

I am astounded at administrators who leave the office without work, in awe at the fact that they can rid their desks of mounds of paperwork during the course of a school day. My daytime hours were spent in the halls and in the classrooms and in the cafeteria during lunch periods. (A colleague of mine from another high school unabashedly claimed, "Lunch period is the most dangerous time of the day, so I would never go in the cafeteria then.") I was visible and accessible to students and staff, including innumerable parent walk-in conferences and phone calls. I chose to do the work this way. It is usually done with the office door shut, with secretaries trained to screen and block intruders. Many educational leadership/management positions have layer upon layer of buffers to prevent access to the top. But the high school principal is looked to from those below and looked at from those above. Ultimately, he or she will be responsible for violence, test scores, poor teachers, bad students, college admissions or rejections, angry parents, graduation rates, toxic materials, slippery hallways, clogged toilets, firecrackers, inadequate supplies, poor morale, drug-dealing, prejudices, cold weather, hot weather, bullying, and overall life and health of school operations.

ETHAN

Ethan walks into my office and slumps down in a chair. It's March, and seniors are on edge waiting for college acceptance letters and classes that must be passed in order to graduate. Ethan is in all advanced placement classes but lately has been cutting physics. I continue typing the last few words of an e-mail without looking up. I go over to the table and sit across from him.

"What is it, Ethan?"

He tells me he just doesn't feel like going to AP physics anymore. "You know, Mrs. Robbin, if I wanted to read a textbook on physics, I would just read the book at night."

The teacher (I know) is in retirement mode; the class is a sleeper. I arrange with his teacher to allow Ethan to complete the year in the course as an "independent study." The teacher asks for a stipend since there will be extra work to grade and extra time to put in to plan independent study projects. I take a study hall duty away from the teacher instead. Ethan is valedictorian, top of his class at Dartmouth, and just completed medical school at Yale.

CHAPTER ELEVEN

Depending upon the school district, and most probably in the State of New York, teacher evaluation forms are, in part, crafted by the "crafty" hands of the teacher unions. In Mason County, I received an annual evaluation from my immediate superior. At Lincoln Center, I witnessed staff being fired, without notice, for lateness, poor attitude with the customers, and excessive absences. In my real estate years, I didn't see any firings, but that's because your earnings dictated the amount of support you received from your affiliated agency. You don't sell, you don't earn. And until you are selling at a credible, sufficient level, there are no perks from the agency. You pay for whatever expenses you incur in the listing, marketing, or selling of a property. As principal of the high school, I never received a formal evaluation from Dr. Carl, although I met with him regularly to discuss the projects, processes, and personnel matters of the moment. I did receive a formal recommendation on my tenure appointment after three years in the district. As a principal, according to the contract, I had to do three evaluations per year on a new teacher; however, if the administrator deemed the teacher satisfactory, he/she could waive the guideline of three evaluations. There was as well a more cumbersome process for dismissing a teacher, particularly if they were tenured.

When I arrived at the high school, several tenured teachers who were also problematic were retiring within a year. I was fortunate to be able to hire many new teachers through the infamous process of shared decision making. For nontenured teachers, when it became evident that it was "not a match," I quite simply told them so. Before any final farewell meeting, I had conducted numerous conferences with the faltering individual. These discussions were private, and the individual was entitled to have a union representative present at the meeting if they so chose. The conference was always prefaced with "This is an informal discussion." Usually—actually, in six out of seven instances—nontenured individuals chose to leave and were (in several of the cases) encouraged to move on by their union reps. These "resignations" were amicable, and people moved on. In my doctoral classes, I wrote a paper on the interview and evaluation process, which could be reduced to three questions:

1. Can they do the job?
2. Will they do the job?
3. Do they fit the organization?

With the exception of one teacher who evidenced on a consistent basis—no control over his classes, primarily due to little or no lesson planning—was there difficulty conveying the message. We spent weeks on "improvement" plans, many documented observations and hours of conversation. When, with the presence of the union rep, I told him it wasn't a match, he was in denial. He had been an adequate substitute for years, and this was his first full teaching job. He was married with four children and the sole support of his family. I was empathetic to his personal situation but uncompromising in my judgment that seven or more months of continuous support by his own colleagues had resulted in no improvement. When the decision was final, and he knew in April he would be terminated in June, he attempted a few ill-fated strategies to change my mind. First, he became obsequious in his gratitude for my counsel. "You're right, I am learning so much from you." Phase two was dropping in well after-school hours when I was alone in my office. He would stand opposite the desk and become wide-eyed and argumentative about why he should remain. Phase three was he would call me at home or be waiting in the parking lot, a now angry and bullying presence. This subsided somewhat when I reminded him I would be the first call made by a potentially new employer for his reference. Not quite a year later, I received a letter from him telling me he was working at a small private elementary school with special education students, and he wanted me to know he had found his niche. He apologized for his behavior and wanted to thank me for helping him move on. I suppose he could have just as easily left in a "shoot-out at the OK Corral" mode had fewer hours been spent listening to his "story." In the book and movie *Up in the Air*, the victims of the pink slip have some knowledge that termination is always possible in the competitive workforce. For teachers, this is almost unheard of, not even on their radar, unless equated with budgetary layoffs.

The teacher evaluation form at Woodland Valley is six pages with rated blocks to check—category after category of skill sets and room for observer comment. Usually all of us were late for the evaluation timeline. But I was the only administrator who addressed seven teachers and one assistant principal and subsequently terminated them for poor performance. There was one teacher, exceptional in every way, for whom I waived more than the suggested number of evaluations. I had worked with him as an outside contracted staff person on the very successful media program. He was certified in English and a master in interdisciplinary instruction and expertly qualified in film, media, and technology. He was hired as soon as an opening occurred in the English department and fast became a popular instructor with a packed schedule of classes. Just prior to graduation (and ask any high school principal what that time is like), Laura scolded administrators at cabinet for late evaluations. Despite the hours of planning and preparation for graduation, I knew she was out for blood. She had already written up several administrators for other issues—whipping us all into her vision of adequately deferential and compliant soldiers. She was most friendly to me, on whom she depended for protocols surrounding her role at graduation. I detailed the ceremony, went over her speaking part, her place in line and on the stage. She asked me to assist her in ordering her robe and hood, and I asked her what the school colors of her doctorate were. In her squeaky squawk voice, she replied, "Oh, of course I have one, but it's packed up somewhere or other—and it won't matter what colors. Whatever you can get at this late date would be fine."

With graduation over, I am drained and exhausted. I plan a week at a lake house outside Saratoga and come in a few days to pack up exams and graduation robes flung around my office left by departing board members.

Laura calls me the morning of my last day before vacation and says, "I want to see you right now, and you may bring your union rep if you like."

"I don't need a union rep, Laura," I deadpan, although in retrospect, it would have been prudent to have a colleague at least witness her "speech" and note the "visual."

"You have not completed all of your evaluations on nontenured teachers, and so I have written you up in a letter which will be placed in your file, and here it is, and you need to sign it to verify that you received a copy." She has delivered this run-on sentence bit of news without taking a breath or looking me in the eye. I take the three-page write-up and, without reading it, sign the last page while replying "Ohhkaaay . . ." She begins to lecture me on the "dearth" of evals over the years and my negligence and noncompliance with the rules. My head is spinning with a quick replay of events since she took office: fast flashes of her number on caller ID, her incessant demands for written memos giving her historical background of programs that she would spew out at board meetings, her time-consuming and useless meetings, charts, and markers and chatter. I point out the only deficit for a nontenured teacher is the one I have known for three years in the media program, well before he was hired, and that there is a "waiver" clause that can be exercised for nontenured exceptional teachers.

"Well, that is *not* how we will do things, and you have the right to a written response if you choose."

I thank her for her time and am proud of myself for having maintained cool eye contact throughout the meeting. Her eyes darted from the write-up to the wall to the write-up to the wall. As I leave through a back stairway and head up to my office, I am thinking, *I don't* fucking *believe this!* I call Rhoda, soon to be assistant superintendent but who is still the administrator association rep, and tell her, "YOU WON'T FUCKING BELIEVE WHAT SHE JUST DID—SHE FUCKING WROTE ME THE FUCK UP!" I go to her office at the elementary school where she is sitting with my AP, soon to take over the elementary principal position I was denied. I walk in, weeks of suppressed rage spilling out in tears and four-letter words.

"I'm *done*!" I say. "FINISHED! I will leave her with her rules and mentally sick shitload of baggage and *fuck her*. She cannot do anything to me. That *stupid* sick *fuck*! I was supposed to be dead by now. What does *she* think she can do to *me*! I built a near perfect school she is quickly dismantling. I have a *verrry* rich husband, and *I don't need her or this job*! She couldn't carry my shoes in Mason County. She wouldn't qualify to cross the border into Mason County. *She's a fucking sham with no background and I am done!*"

Sam and Rhoda sit wide-eyed and silent. I've never been this hurt or angry. My integrity, my ethics are untouchable, but I am just so tired. Rhoda calls the union attorney for administrators. Within a day, his response is, "We've got her by the balls. She's given you an 'illegal' memo due to some of the 'insubordination' language used."

Great, thanks for nothing. I am already moving mentally to my first vision of the lake, serene and quiet, reflecting the surrounding tall pines. My car is packed, and I tell my husband, who is coming within two days, I will see him soon. I drive the sixty-five miles north replaying her bird-squawking lecture, focused on moving on and out—leaving teachers and students I love, feeling guilty to abandon them, but knowing she's crossed a line with me. I have no choice. I won't defend and subject myself. She read my file, she knows my work, and she even embedded some of my own words and phrases in her speeches. She complimented me on my shoes, invited me out for a "glass of wine" (boundary breaches)—stupidity. She knows who I am and hates who I am. I don't hate her (I think as I approach Exit 13 on the Northway), but she will never leave me alone—it is her or me, and I am deciding I am out of here. Within weeks of Rhoda leaving, I follow her out the door as I am hired as principal of the Cornwall County Institute's

Alternative School—bad kids from ten surrounding districts, and they want me. I take a thirty-thousand-dollar pay cut, give up a lifetime of paid health benefits for myself and my husband, abdicate my tenure status, and kiss good-bye a big accumulated sick leave check I would have received at retirement from the district. Oh well. I guess I showed them.

When I return from vacation, Laura holds an "administrative advance" (her twist on an administrative retreat) at a local bed and breakfast facility. She begins with one of her inane lectures, and I am struck at the anesthesized look on the faces of my colleagues. She dispenses with me fast enough, announcing that I will be leaving by the end of August. With her assistant's help, she passes out five-inch thick laminated black binders, filled, totally packed, with eight-by-eleven paper. We roll our eyes at one another, unable to imagine its content. The binders contain cartoons, printed in colored ink, full pages taken up with only a four-word educational platitude, charts of irrelevant information pulled randomly from the Internet, data pertaining to nothing relevant to our district. The expense in copying alone is mind-boggling. This lady is way out there and over her head. The administrators are mute as Laura asks one by one to read a page aloud. Rhoda scrapes her chair on the slate floor as she pushes back from the table and excuses herself for the restroom. I know I have made the right decision.

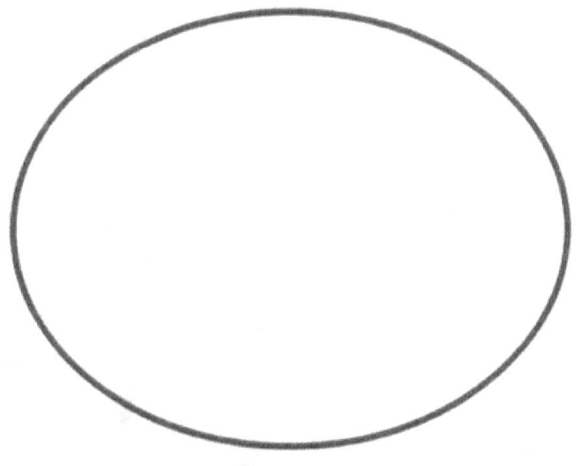

Radiating
Possibility!!

The Belly and the Members

One fine day, it occurred to the Members of the Body that they were doing all the work and the Belly was having all the food.

So they held a meeting, and after a long discussion, decided to strike work till the Belly consented to take its proper share of the work.

So for a day or two, the Hands refused to take the food, the Mouth refused to receive it, and the Teeth had no work to do.

But after a day or two the Members began to find that they themselves were not in a very active condition: the Hands could hardly move, and the Mouth was all parched and dry, while the Legs were unable to support the rest.

So thus they found that even the Belly in its dull quiet way was doing necessary work for the Body, and that all must work together or the Body will go to pieces.

LEARN MORE

Use the questions below to structure a discussion on the promise and peril of population and demographic trends. We offer some suggested sources to complement your consideration of these important issues.

Discussion Questions

1) What exposures—from retiring baby boomers in the U.S. to a graying China to the massive overhang of Europe's elderly—do private corporations, governments, and other sectors have to worry about as the aging revolution unfolds across the globe? How will changing demographics impact workforce composition? Retirement age? Pension outlays? Taxation? Immigration? Economic growth? How can governments, corporations, and nongovernmental organizations work together to address these issues?

Center for Strategic and International Studies 1800 K Street NW, Washington DC 20006
Tel. (202) 887-0200 / www.csis.org / www.7revs.csis.org
© 2006 by the Center for Strategic and International Studies. All rights reserved.

What Can I Do Today?

✓ Turn off classroom lights after special events and after cleaning.
✓ Turn off computers, printers, and copiers at the end of each day.
✓ Change air filters regularly.
✓ Optimize boiler controls. Blue flames and correct air-fuel mix is critical.
✓ Remove unnecessary refrigerators, microwaves, toaster ovens, and coffee pots.
✓ Check and calibrate thermostats and temperature sensors for accurate operation.
✓ Reduce nighttime setbacks to sixty to sixty-two degrees Fahrenheit.
✓ Set responsible heating and AC settings.
✓ Increase nighttime temperature setbacks.
✓ Check all outside doors and windows for weather seals.
✓ Do not open windows or doors for ventilation during cold periods. Adjust ventilation system instead.
✓ Recaulk all open outside masonry cracks.

Contractually, a superintendent can hold a principal sixty days beyond the notification of a resignation, so Laura could have kept me until October. She agreed to let me go after the first two days of school. The first day was Superintendent's Conference Day. The second was when the students returned. She wanted me to be there to tell the students, classroom by classroom, that I was leaving and introduce them to Dave, who had been called back, now as the interim principal (only at $550 per diem) until a permanent hire. On Conference Day, all staff members for the district convened in the auditorium for her opening, rallying welcome. She introduced new people and announced there would be some changes. She told them about my new position and asked me to come up to receive a huge bouquet of flowers. As I approached the microphone where she was standing, she asked me in a whisper if I wanted to say anything. I turned away from her and took the microphone to face my audience. Someone later said I should have seen her face throughout my brief words of gratitude and farewell. "I know, I know," I began, "you're all disappointed you won't get to see my new fall line of shoes." When I finished, I was shocked at the thunderous standing ovation. People were standing and crying, and they wouldn't stop. I took my bouquet and walked up the aisle out of the auditorium to my office where I promptly dumped the flowers in my trash can, cellophane and all. The next day, we moved from class to class, and Dave told some jokes after being introduced by me as their interim.

Some kids gasped, some groaned, and others were just silent.

Chapter Twelve

I am about to embark on an experience in education that will add a priceless dimension to a learning curve I felt I had more than completed. It will be the most challenging of all my years put together: I will meet individuals whose value to me is worth more than any salary with compounded benefits. I will close the gap in knowing the formula for reforming high schools and will need, and draw upon every minute and ounce of experience, education and energy from all my years on earth to meet this challenge. I will emerge with wisdom and confidence I no longer need to question, nor can it be second-guessed by others. I will laugh more than I have ever laughed in my life, and I will finally be ready to tell this story.

ISAIAH

Isaiah is biracial and moved to New York from Arizona with his single-parent mother. She is a crack addict. I knew him at fourteen years old when I was principal at Woodland Valley. One morning (which was also Isaiah's first day at Woodland), I got stuck behind a school bus. I saw the bus stop for Isaiah, who was standing along the road at the end of a long driveway. The bus pulled away, and Isaiah was left right where he had been standing. I pulled up to him and rolled down the window and asked him what happened.

He said, "I'm not on his list."

"Aren't you new? And isn't this your first day?"

Isaiah nodded, head bowed, clearly embarrassed.

"Well, you're in luck, I'm the principal, and I'm here to take you to school myself."

He slid into the front seat of the Audi, and we drove back to his house so he could tell his mother. He returned to the car and said, "It's all right. She's still sleeping." I meet Isaiah again at age seventeen at the alternative school. He is forbidden on Woodland Valley School property and tells me it is because of his "anger" issues. He becomes Rudy's sous-chef in the cooking elective and successfully completes the GED program and passes the series of exams. He has made dramatic gains, works around the school and grounds in the internship program, and has shown an interest in investing his money. I have just finished *Snowball*, the story of Warren Buffet, and tell him how Mr. Buffet started out by saving pennies. Isaiah asks to borrow the book, which is a very thick paperback. He arrives at school each day with the book proudly tucked under his arm.

CHAPTER THIRTEEN

The gold Murano pulls into a space in front of an auto bay at the Cornwall County Institute, clearly marked No Parking, and giving me an unobstructed view from the window of my new office. Alexis Ballister Conlon high-steps around the rear of the car and opens the back door. She's tall with perfect long legs, sporting four-inch heels and a low-cut silky dress number that ends midthigh. She emerges from the backseat with a baby and a pink canvas bag of essentials slung over one shoulder—a Coach (is that a Coach?) leather tote on the other. My new boss, three years older than my daughter, enters the building with a flourish. Although I met her during my interview, she immediately took her summer vacation at their beach house in Outer Banks, so I have not seen her since. She brings the baby to the in-house day care and goes up the stairs to her suite of offices without stopping in to see how my first day is going.

My new secretary asks if I want her to answer my phone and take messages and sort through and open my mail. "Yes to all," I reply. Two minutes later, my phone rings . . . and rings (she is in the adjoining office where one has to pass to get to my landlocked space). I pick up. "Good morning, this is Barbara Robbin." So begins the precedent of her not doing any of the things she offered to do. Gordon, my new AP, wanders in to "brief" me on how things are around here. He's friendly and talkative, and within ten minutes, I know he is from some small town south of Buffalo. He rents an apartment in a complex where one of the students (who is real bad news) lives, but he hopes I'll agree with his opinion to put the kid in "placement" (short for juvenile lockup facility). He has a pudgy face and has been steadily eating candy from a bowl I filled with Life Savers and set in the middle of my conference table. As he begins a discourse on the state of his finances, my secretary—who has been coming to the door and peering through the half-glass window and obviously becoming more and more agitated—opens the door with her key and breathlessly exclaims, "Excuse me for interrupting your meeting, but somebody has to unlock the bus doors!" It is now eight o'clock, and Gordon has consumed the first hour of my day.

I visit each class—there are only about twenty—and introduce myself to the teachers and students. I am amazed at the amount of technology each room is equipped with. Students have their own desktops, and there are smart boards with ceiling-mounted projectors. The rooms are spacious, and with a special education class capped at six and an alternative class no bigger than twelve and no rooms that have to be shared, this is a surprising luxury. During one of the three lunch periods, I approach a table with five black girls, and one sends me a drop-dead, whadda-ya-lookin'-at-girl look just in case I misconstrue the message that I am unwelcomed in their "space." I introduce myself in this one-way exchange and slowly move to another table, but notice they give my shoes a second look. The student-to-staff ratio is very small. There are teaching assistants in every room, one-on-one aides for students who need extra supervision, three crisis workers, two guidance counselors, four social workers, two psychiatrists, a school resource officer, six clerical and two administrators. There is an underlying tension among students as they move every forty minutes to new classes, and the occasional "Fuck you, bitch" is immediately quelled by aides or crisis staff. Some teachers are warm and friendly, but most are unsmiling, skeptical, and range from young to should-be-retired-by-now in age. They are models for fashion don'ts, sporting cargo shorts and Hawaiian-print shirts, short skirts revealing high-carb legs, and skintight tops with plunging necklines. One wears a perfume or body cream so pungent, it permeates the air within a twenty-foot radius, and I will be plagued for years with her no-warning hugs that leave my clothes saturated. I have two prize guidance counselors in Evie and Evan. Evie is twenty-eight, beautiful and exuberant and newly engaged to the man of her dreams. She is funny and can do the California-girl dialect when she imitates the kids in her "girls'" group or when she is relaying a conversation with a teacher complaining about a new student she has placed in their class. She is a supreme multitasker, scheduling, counseling, and arranging test schedules and duty assignments. She takes students out for runs along the river in good weather and sits right down at the table in the cafeteria and eats her lunch with the students. Evan is thirty-four, back a few years from a tour in Iraq and a new father to a baby girl. He is unruffled. Teachers can get right up in his face and accuse him of "undermining" them by "always taking sides with the student," and Evan doesn't flinch. He tells me once you have been in Iraq, the rest of the life as we know it just falls into perspective. Evan, like Evie, interacts with the students, and the basketball court is as much a venue for counseling as is his office.

The students go out and smoke along the highway in front of O'Mara's general store. They return at their leisure, picking and choosing what classes to attend. There are apparent factions between white and black students and between blacks and Hispanics. The girls are tough and streetwise. If something crosses their impulsive and flighty minds, they say it. "Whadthefuckyouthinkyoudoingirl," no diction, grammar, no sense of purpose, just there. By the third day, at bus dismissal, where all students board their buses bound for any one of ten districts, some as far as forty miles away, the radios crackle, "Fight on 27!" I am closest to the bus and head for its back door where two bodies are pressed tightly against the emergency door, locked in a choke hold, legs flailing. The student passengers are leaning over the backs of seats, shouting, swearing, and cheering them on when I hear on my radio, "I got it, Ms. Ro." Within seconds, Rudy, one of the crisis workers, has opened the back door of the bus while JT, the other crisis worker, has already entered the bus from the front, and the boys are quickly separated. As they continue shouting obscenities and threats, Rudy leads one back into the building, and Gordon calls the parent. Staff disperse and go home. Gordon stays with the kid until his ride comes. No one seems to think this is a notable event, but my adrenaline is pumping.

Alexis occupies the penthouse, a suite of offices at the top of the stairs on the second floor, with two secretaries and her own business manager. Her office takes up the space of what would be three classrooms and includes an oval conference table; built-in bookshelves; a kitchenette area with refrigerator, stove, and sink; and a wall-mounted flat-screen TV. I enter her office promptly at 3:00 PM for our first supervisors' meeting (although I am the first of three to arrive), and she waves me in as she continues to talk to her husband on the phone (I feel like the older woman in *The Devil Wears Prada*, only the roles are reversed. I am standing before the thirty-something ingenue, waiting for my turn for her attention.) She completes the call with her fingers scrolling through messages on her Blackberry and her computer, shouting for her secretary, "ELAINE, EELAAINE—chop-chop! I need the Pine Meadow referral!" I am stunned at her energy, fast and loud talking—like a tornado touching down, wreaking havoc, swirling back up, and touching back down again. She doesn't seem at all interested in the "business of today" as much as she is telling me about their trip to Carolina and the antics of her two—and six-year-olds with a sprinkling of comments about her husband, Rodney. There are colored stick figure drawings from Gabby and Eliza where they have written "I love my mom" and painted smiles on the sun. The supervisors from the other satellite sites arrive: BK and Connie, along with Gordon—who crosses the room to the table—and I pretend not to notice, his pants are stuck in the crack of his ass. Alexis has a glass-pedestal candy dish on the table filled with Pep-O-Mints that Gordon begins to almost unconsciously devour. Connie unwraps the paper on hers, bites off a small piece, and chews it slowly and deliberately before taking a second bite. BK doesn't touch them but has been talking nonstop since she entered the room. Alexis finally comes out from behind her desk and brings a huge pile of stapled packets of paper. "This is for you," she says as she places the pile in front of me. "And this." And another half-inch stapled packet is put on the top of my pile. They are referrals, documenting sixteen or so years of the life of a failed student and include psycho-educational testing, medications, hospitalizations, court appearances, type of learning disability, transcripts, and the social family history and narrative of family dynamics—sexually abused by an uncle, alcoholic father, crack mother who caused trauma beating child with a hairbrush, CPS involvement, CCS, DSS, etc. BK continues in her one run-on sentence rant. "And I said to Lou [the principal in the building where her program is housed] at seven o'clock, when we were both still in the building and just processing the day, how I told the parent we would not tolerate the biting behavior despite his medication adjustments, and I *know* how restraints are done." Alexis continues sorting through her mail pile, discarding some envelopes, occasionally putting a colored flyer in the middle of the table and interrupting BK to say, "Anyone want to go to this conference in Denver on dealing with difficult parents?" BK hasn't taken a breath, Gordon is on his sixth mint, and Connie folds her hands in front of her, and I pretend to be absorbed in a referral packet and do not have a clue as to what is going on. By 3:45 PM (forty-five minutes into this meeting), Alexis's papers have been either discarded or redistributed to the four of us. "Rodney's mother is such a *bitch*!" she exclaims. "I don't want my kids around them anymore. Any problems today? How were your openings?" Before anyone has a chance to answer, Alexis abruptly gets up and goes to the refrigerator and comes back with a bottle of water and an orange she begins to peel. Gordon attempts a few jokes about the staff. "Anyone want water?" Alexis asks while twisting the cap on her bottle. BK is still talking. By 5:00 PM, Alexis looks at me and says, "You can go home now." I quickly fill my purse with pen and glasses, pack up the referrals, and slide on my coat. No one else has moved. As I wave good-night, I pass by Elaine, who is still at her desk with piles of paper in neat stacks all around her. I have that vacant, almost homesick feeling in my stomach. I miss the teachers at Woodland, I miss the students with normal speech, and I miss their social skills. I slip into the pace of traffic. I need my home, my white bedroom, my fresh air, my brilliant husband (who won't believe a word of what I will tell him), and I need to call my beautiful children.

As I walk in the door, I receive a call from Linda, the Woodland business manager.

"Hi, Barb! I'm calling to do the exit interview. I just have a few questions to ask you."

My head is pounding—I'm exhausted and starving and numb from the past few days of roller-coaster emotions.

Linda continues. "Were you satisfied with your employment?"

"Yes."

"Did you leave on your own volition?"

"Yes."

"Did you feel there was any discrimination in the way you were treated?"

"Yes."

"Oh, that's not good, Barb."

What the fuck! Is she worried I'll sue? For what?

"Well, good luck, Barb. I'll have your check for accumulated vacation leave ready."

(Yeah, and since that is somewhat negotiable, is that my carrot? I figure it's around $7,000, which seems miniscule compared to the 30K cut-in pay and the lifetime health benefits I've given up.)

The next day, I meet Linda, who hands me a check for $24,342. Wearily I look at the check and hand it back to her. "It's wrong, Linda."

"Oh no, this is what it amounts to," she says and hands me back the check, insulted that I have questioned her calculations.

"No, Linda, it's not that much."

She sighs heavily and obviously just wants me to go away. She takes out her "Barbara" file and, using her calculator, makes a series of clicking noises as her fingers fly over the keys and comes up with the lesser amount. "Ohhhh . . . ," she replies. "Ohhhhh . . . we will have to reissue another check."

I walk to my car in the parking lot, wondering how many errors have been made in severance funds—how many teachers and administrators have brought them to the attention of the business manager and, three times, requested them to check the figures.

The days and weeks are on fast-forward. Within the first year, we bring in my friend for the intensive dance workshop, who leads students solely with her expertise in capturing their attention and harnessing their energy through movement. Forty-five students participate in her self-help sharing discussions, exploring the meaning of attention, equating it to love, empathizing with their solitude and misery, tapping into abused souls, and putting it to the music of Marvin Gaye and Whitney Houston. At the final performance held in the gym (where there have never been assemblies), three separate groups perform. Their limbs move in perfect synchronization. Teachers are stunned at the rowdy, undisciplined, impulsive troublemakers who are performing flawlessly before their peers. Alexis brings her two-year-old, who sits on her lap. Bud Snow, the superintendent, Assistant Rhoda, and central office staff attend. A teacher remarks that she has never seen students learn so quickly and give such attention to the workshop.

Four young nontenured teachers approach me one late afternoon to tell me Gordon makes them "uncomfortable." He stands too closely to them, looks at them leeringly, and occasionally "just grabs his crotch." (This I have noticed myself.) I report this to Alexis, who speaks with them separately and asks that they document these incidents. They refuse, frightened that he can jeopardize their tenure recommendations. Gordon stays hours after school. He preys on single mothers, commiserates with the tough boys they have to handle, and makes promises he will help "send them away." He invades personal space—students call him an "asshole" to his face, and he continues to follow them down the halls, revving their anger, whining, "I'm nice to youuuu . . . Why do youuuu call me naaames . . ." I discover his checkered career path. He cruises through the days, burying himself in CSE meetings where he can talk and talk.

Sometimes, he even cries as he brings up his own soppy history of irrelevant events. He negotiates "placements" for the kids who have called him the worst names. He jokes too familiarly with one of the girls and touches the side of her leg. She tells me Mr. Davis makes her feel uncomfortable. I envision him in his apartment, gorging himself on junk food in his underwear and searching porn sites or Facebook on the young teachers. He is a predator, and I make up my mind I will make the case for no-tenure appointment, since he is only in his second year.

My secretary resembles Cruella from *101 Dalmatians*. She has long dark hair to her waist with naturally dry and brittle curls. I walk into her office and find her hair flung over her head and onto the desk. Deputy Dole is massaging her shoulders and neck. They do not seem at all uncomfortable at my intrusion on my way to my own office but break it up as I pass them. I see them together often, eating at a picnic bench behind the building, talking in her office with blinds closed and surrounded by tropical "little shop of horrors" plants. In the morning, she is in early and sometimes surprises me when I come in her dark office and assume she is not there. "I leave the lights off so no one will bother me," she says the first time she startles me. It is a huge annoyance to her that I keep my office door open and allow students and teachers to come in unannounced. She snaps out shrill comments at random and once pointed a finger at me prefacing her comment with "We don't *do* things that way around here!" I ignore her outbursts as she can turn on a dime and suddenly, in a hushed and whispery childlike voice, tell me "how wonderful" I am. In no time, she confides that she is the sole support of her mother who just "picks, picks, picks at me" about all she does wrong. Sometimes we go days without speaking—she locks the outer door to her office (effectively keeping people from getting to mine), and I unlock it. She microwaves soups and sauces in plastic containers for her lunch, and I am embarrassed at the junk appliances, plants, paper, and overall crap that greet anyone who enters the principal's office. I speak with Alexis about transferring her. I have found dozens of referrals stacked under her desk, waiting to reach my desk for processing. This results in huge delays in new student intakes and tuition revenues. I propose a streamlined referral process that will bypass her desk completely on the grounds that the districts are complaining about the time it takes to get a "kid" in to our program. Alexis has already been consulting with her about me. It is easy to figure out, based on what snippets each of them tell me, that my every move is being monitored. Communication is so circular and chaotic, and the chain of command is as specific as it is ignored. It will take three years to transfer my secretary to another site, during which time, she will do little work and create tension I will spend time and energy neutralizing every day.

During the first summer, seventeen members of the staff sign up for summer curriculum work (for which they are paid $500 stipends). We meet as a group, and they are shocked at being able to select their own topics for school improvement, work individually or in small groups, and make their own time and place meeting schedules. They no longer are required to sign in at faculty meetings, and one teacher tells me for the first time in ten years, she feels "trusted." Faculty meetings have been thematic. I bring in articles about other alternative programs, statistics on the changing population of alternative students. I always stress the importance of their work and the potential of building a model program that might even make a *60 Minutes* segment. They listen with rapt attention and seem energized at the prospects of being a part of something grand. Many come to my office to tell me they support these efforts, to tell me how "on board" they are with the changes, yet they are never vocal in the meetings. There is the proverbial rep, who also shadows my door and tells me the new schedule will put us out of compliance with special education regulations.

We amicably debate the efficiency of offering interdisciplinary curriculum with collaborative teaching teams. She tells me with a constant smile on her face, "You won't win this." I find out much later that the rep has weekly off-site "coffee" meetings with Rhoda. Rhoda's information is now going through the rep's filter, not mine, and not even Alexis's.

This is a broken staff. Alternative education is often a dumping ground for the least skilled teachers when, in fact, it should demand only those with the highest level of skill and talent. The alternative population, largely, will either pay off the most or cost the taxpayer the most. Much of this staff have been here many years; now so vested in the New York State pension system, they are hanging on for the lifetime payout. There is no incentive for changing your outdated methodology, no punishment if you choose to come in and pop a DVD in the machine for students to watch while you read the paper, and you are paid if you are sick eighteen days (for which there will be a paid substitute) out of a 180-day school year. You don't have to navigate icy roads when schools are closed, and you can grieve your administration if you teach too many classes or go without a duty-free lunch. You just have to "last." Many of these teachers do not come close to the "bar." Their résumés end up in the preliminary cut at high-performing schools. Their career path has too many jumps and starts. Their essays rife with misspellings or grammatical errors. When they make it in here, they have to develop a tolerance for four-letter words and kids who occasionally punch a wall or have a cigarette. But these teachers have their own natural tolerance for mediocrity. They seem to identify with the students. They too were the black sheep in their families whose parents (if there were parents) didn't extend trust or confidence in their futures, weren't all that involved in their growth. Perhaps there was a history of alcoholism or domestic violence or drug abuse, though not sufficient enough to inspire so much as fatigue and numb. So a teacher here finds camaraderie. It is a comfort zone in which he or she could not be discovered or caught at their own inadequacy. It provides the income to support their "real lives" with dysfunctional partners, disappointing children, and the stage on which to act out the pain of all that they had been denied. It was, in fact, the perfect storm conditions for a problem-school dynamic.

Teachers were about to undergo a shift in public perception from being largely ignored to overly scrutinized. As my staff went through the motions of doing their summer curriculum work, they were ambivalent about change. My job was to create a culture for "safe" change—change that would eliminate the fear of being exposed for what they were while helping the most disadvantaged kids in the area.

With a compilation of work turned in by the teachers, much of which had been googled and copied from the Internet, I put together a proposal that represented, at least, a fresh start to a stagnating program. Now, with some teams of teachers, the ninth-period electives—which included debate, arts and crafts, and cooking—and the student government, we obtained permission from Rhoda and Buddy to add the successful film and media program I had used at Woodland Valley. With Willy at the helm, a master of integrating technology with academic curriculum, students began developing their own websites on the Civil War battles and putting their poetry to music. The year actually flourished. Enrollment increased dramatically. Woodland Valley seemed to be emptying the building with all the students they sent to alternative for what seemed to be minor infractions. Zero tolerance in bad behavior was the mantra, and elevating test scores, the ultimate goal.

The second year, we were able to hire two new teachers. Gordon continued to offset progress made with students, but he was "looking" for another position closer to Buffalo. His absences increased to incorporate résumé writing and interviews. He told me about all the "near hits" and how impressed people were with him, but to no avail. By April, Alexis and I had decided to let him know he would not be recommended for tenure.

I chose the morning, and when he came into my office as he usually did, I said, "I have something to tell you."

To which he replied, "And I have something to tell *you*!"

"You go first," I said.

He was selected to be the new principal of a small rural school, negligibly closer to Buffalo, but we were free. When Alexis bounded in, I cut her off quickly. "Gordon has the most wonderful news to tell us!"

For weeks into his new position, he called to tell me how well he was doing, how good the food was at the meetings, and how he set an orderly, no-nonsense tone for the small body of rural students. I noticed the unflushed toilet with urine on the rim of the bowl with the seat left up in the coed staff restroom ceased since he left.

RICO

Rico has been in the program only a few months. He's five feet, maybe an inch or two taller, slight build, which makes him look shrunken in the black leather jacket he wears all year round. Behind every theft—iPod, cell phone, gym shorts—somewhere in the drug deals that go down, or in an exchange of money, Rico's name always surfaces. JT and Rudy make him empty his pockets on my conference table. Rico then holds up his arms (like he's familiar with these pat downs); he removes his sneakers, which reveal blackened, once-white socks. The table holds a semicrushed Marlboro, a lighter, a thick blue magic marker, his Latin King do-rag, and a phone number scratched out on a piece of paper. Nothing. The seventeen-year-old transplant from East Harlem sits confidently in the chair and says, "Ahhhhh, c'mon, Ms. Ro, I don't got nothin'." Rudy removes the cap to the marker and smells the length of the plastic and pops out a roll of marijuana. Rico defeatedly throws his head backward, hitting the window. "Awwwhhhh . . ." He's suspended five days, and while Deputy Dole processes his court appearance ticket, he waits in my office, and I ask him what he will do the next five days.

"Probably work in the slaughterhouse, they pay $11.50 an hour."

"What do you do?" I ask.

"Kill rabbits," he replies. "Wanna know how I do it, Ms. Ro? First, I slit the throat and let the blood run out . . ."

I listen without expression as he mesmerizes me with his cold, matter-of-fact recipe for preparing rabbit meat for sale.

Maxine, the CCS worker, drives him home. He tells her to let him out, that his house is just around the corner as they reach the center of town.

"Oh no," she says. "I'm takin' you to your front door." Rico directs her down a few side streets to a patch of dirt and overgrown weeds where a battered trailer sits on top of concrete blocks. A line of cable stretches from the roof to a nearby power line. Rico opens the car door, steps out, and shuts the door. He then leans back in the window and thanks her for the ride.

Chapter Fourteen

By August, we interviewed a new AP. Our first choice was a football-type statuesque African American from a small urban district to the south of us. Lenny was exactly what we were looking for. He was insightful, nonconfrontational, knowledgeable about inner city tough kids, and funny. There was a second candidate—young, long red hair worn in a ponytail, still working on his administrative certification, so charismatic and smart, so engaging and outrageous that Alexis and I wanted both of them. We were able to hire Lenny and get "the Kid" two days a week as an intern.

The media program had expanded to include a community school component. Willy took on ten of the most difficult students who did not attend any classes and who could erupt on a second's notice. Many of the incoming referrals described students with violent and psychiatrically involved backgrounds. But with Willy, these same kids would sit for hours on end as he taught them sound engineering, did GED preparation work, and listened to their stories. The level of technology being used was astounding. Rep kept up her backstabbing sabotage and continued her meetings with Rhoda. Rhoda popped in once unannounced and walked around the building. "There's only ten kids in there," she quipped when she passed Willy's community school. "And one is sleeping. What really does he do?" I do not miss the fact that she is echoing the rep from the most recent coffee klatch. She totally misses the fact that all ten of these kids should be in residential placement costing districts hundreds of thousands of dollars, except for the fact that we have miraculously engaged them in learning. Willy, as low-key, diplomatic, and unthreatening as he is, has gotten attention by getting the attention of the most challenging students in the building. I try to explain but am met with a dismissive, sarcastic smile. The dynamic between Rhoda and me has shifted dramatically since our days on Dr. Carl's council. She is clearly conveying the message that I am her subordinate, and perhaps, since I too was a candidate for the assistant position (never interviewed, but after all, she does have her doctorate), I pose somewhat of a threat to her.

Lenny, the Kid, Alexis, and I are undaunted. We will prevail, concentrating on the new teachers, including Dominic Spellini, whose energy surpasses all of ours put together. We have Evie and Evan and Rudy and JT and some cutting-edge veteran people. We name ourselves "the inner circle."

Unlike the lead management style of Dr. Carl, which I have not seen since I last saw him, Cornwall County Institute is a highly bureaucratic organization. Great for an automobile assembly plant. Principals were too low in the hierarchy to attend weekly cabinet meetings at central office. "Gonna go to Disneyland," Alexis would chirp every Thursday morning. The result was diluted representation from the building level. Alexis often referred to her job as director as totally separate from my role as principal. The irony was her assignments were the same as mine at Woodland Valley as well as the ones I assumed at the building level. The extra layer of bureaucracy and the additional filter for information from building level to superintendent ensured—at best, ambivalent alliances and skewed, self-preserving communication.

One afternoon, I answer my phone (as usual), "Good afternoon, this is Barbara Robbin."

And I hear, "Hi, Barbara, this is Moira Smith, president of the board of education in the Woodland Valley district."

Although I had read numerous second-page articles in the local paper about the disgruntled state of affairs in that district and the resignations of several board members, I never looked back when I left. She wanted historical information about the media program that was up for a budget cut and asked if I could answer some questions about my experience with the program—how it started, number of students it served. We chatted about ten minutes, and she said, "You must have been wonderful to work with." Coincidentally, a few days later, I received a call from Cindy (my friend who brought the program to us), whose husband had passed away many months earlier. I told her, whenever she was ready, we would arrange a girls' night out. She said she was ready for our outing, and we arranged to meet one evening at a restaurant that she and her husband had frequented. While we waited for a table (it was packed that night), several people who knew her and several who knew me came up to say hello. One was a parent of one of my students from Woodland Valley, and he wanted to tell me all about his daughter and how she was doing at college. Cindy talked for most of the evening, telling me about her wrenching last days with her husband. She had been one of seven students accepted to do a special research project at Columbia on teenagers' susceptibility to rejection and how that affected their ability to learn. My alternative students couldn't have been a more perfect population to study. It would involve some grad students administering a questionnaire and spending a few days at the site. To me, it was a no-brainer. The talk about data-based research to justify programs and personnel and learning strategies was all the rage at instructional trainings. This was an opportunity from an Ivy League school to obtain research to use in developing a model for alternative students based on predictable behaviors that teachers would have to recognize and adapt their instruction accordingly.

Examples of typical student-teacher interactions are the following:

1. Student arrives at classroom door. Teacher greets student with scowl on face, hands on hips, and quips, "Why are you late?"

Student responds, "I was getting breakfast."

Teacher says, "Well, you've had enough time and shouldn't be late, so go to REO" (in-school suspension / holding room).

Student responds, "Fuck you, this is bullshit," and kicks the door as he leaves.

2. Student is in class and distracting other students upon being presented with a packet of work. Teacher says, "Malcolm, stop being disruptive."

Malcolm says, "Wha'd *I do*?"

Teacher says, "You know, now settle down."

Malcolm cracks a joke for his audience of peers.

Teacher says, "That's it, leave the room *now*."

Malcolm says, "No, I didn't *do* anything."

Teacher picks up the phone and calls front desk and says, "Send crisis to remove Malcolm from room 102."

JT

"Awwright . . ." In a slow, Southern drawl, JT answers to a frantic call on the radio that there is a crisis in room 206. He is near the staircase, and I see him move up the steps at his regular pace, unrushed. When he gets to the doorway of 206, he already knows it's Chantel. When she sees him, she stops what has been a steady stream of curses directed at another girl. The teacher rapidly relays the background information to JT, who has already, with a slight nod, gotten Chantel to pack up her stuff and head toward the door where he is still standing. "Stephanie called her a skank, and she just exploded, JT, and then the papers went flying, and I almost had to get between them . . . and . . . really, Chantel was verrry threatening . . . and it is a saaafety issue . . ."

JT doesn't say a word. He walks down the hall with Chantel, who is now pleading her defense to him. "*She* started it, JT, an' I ain't goin' to REO. She's a fuckin' bitch an I'm gonna fight her. This ain't faaaairrr."

When they get to the reorientation room, Chantel is still talking, and JT says, "Sit down!"

"Ahhh, c'mon, JT, you know you love me . . ." And she takes her seat.

JT goes back to the desk and continues to read his e-mail. The room is quiet.

JT is an African American, the baby in a family of nine siblings. He calls himself a mama's boy. When all the others left home to start their families and seek their fortunes (two went on to become major league baseball players), JT stayed in his hometown, started his own family, and looked after his mother. He works two jobs, has a beautiful wife, two kids—one son, a straight-A as well as an athletic student, and a three-year-old daughter, the only one in the family who has him wrapped around her finger.

JT has been a crisis worker at alternative for seven years and one of three African Americans on the staff (the other two being student aides). His very presence will stop a rumble in the making. He is a role model and mentor; he exudes the quiet confidence of one as secure with himself as he is sure of his capabilities. He is the silent force that keeps the students and the school safe. JT can "read" people, kids or adults, in a glance and be right. He knows every single schedule for every student and every teacher. He knows who is out of area and who is in class. He knows who just left the boys' room and who just blew up in the cafeteria. He knows every bus—their route, driver, and the time of their arrival and departure. He shoots baskets with students during their lunch periods and doesn't miss the precursors to a heated quarter. He doesn't commiserate or sympathize; he just understands them and will not allow them to make excuses for any reason. JT has wit and humor and insight that can match the best of the best. He and Rudy complement each other. They are the dream team.

"Hey, Ru, where you at?"

"Hey, J, your location . . ."

They speak in code and act in tandem, covering necessary ground in split seconds, appearing and disappearing as the conditions require. "Professional" is coming to work every day and being prepared—overprepared, expertly prepared, knowing your subject inside and out. JT is a professional.

When Cornwall Institute cut the budget this year, "last one in, first one out" applied according to union dictates. JT is excessed. A crisis worker with more longevity will be transferred to the site. He is known for his sarcasm and confrontational, bullying approach. Despite the appeals on behalf of JT, the contract will prevail. As notice of the layoffs are given to staff, the gamut of emotion range from tears to anger. JT is nonplussed. He makes a few calls to line up new work and keeps coming in every day and doing his job.

Our last day together, JT says, "I think somethin' bad's gonna happen, Miz Ro."

CHAPTER FIFTEEN

A meeting is set up among Cindy, Rhoda, Alexis, and me to discuss the research project. Dr. Rhoda seems to support the initiative, and we all break into big smiles that we can proceed. "Whoa, whoa, whoa," she says as though she is astride a runaway horse. "The *next* step is to *discuss* this with Buddy."

A week later, Alexis returns from her cabinet meeting and enters my office like a locomotive.

"*Medialert* is *gone!*"

"What do you mean?" I say.

"*I mean gone* . . . g-on-e—like in *over!*"

"When?" I ask.

"*Now.*"

"You mean like today?"

"I mean, like give Willy and the crew notice and a week to get their stuff out."

"*Why?*" I say. It's just beginning to sink in she is serious.

"There's *no more* money!"

"What about the ten kids in community school and the nineteen in the elective class?"

"They'll have to do something else."

"Like *what*?" I push back.

"I don't know, figure it out, and by the way, Dr. Rhoda made a comment that 'Barbara should watch out who she socializes with!' and Buddy said some board member made a comment at a Woodland Valley board meeting that they had talked to you in *person*!"

Medialert was pulled out—computers shut down; kids funneled back into classes they did not need or hung out at O'Mara's. The frigid treatment from central office continued until April on Superintendent's Conference Day. I saw Buddy leave the gym right after his series of jokes (he and Dave shared the same ones) and asked if I could speak with him. He looked somewhat surprised but followed me to my office. "I'd like to clear up anything you might feel has created this impasse and tension."

"You shouldn't be talking to board members, and we don't do business with people who demean us at public board meetings."

"I don't know what was done at the Woodland Valley board meeting or what was said."

"They said Cornwall Institute costs too much and they could save money by keeping media up there."

"Wellll, that's true, but it has nothing to do with what the program is doing here."

"They can't treat us this way!"

"Buddy, I think this is a mistake, and it will have a negative effect on our students."

"You'll figure something out. Well, I'm glad we talked, or it would have just festered."

In one fell swoop, with backdoor, back-stabbing, misinformed gossip, the Medialert program and the research study were gone. Nineteen elective students suffered, and of the ten community school students, three were sent to residential institutions at a cost of $100,000 per student for their districts. Two students dropped out of school. Calvin still rides his bike aimlessly along Route 222, uneducated but smart, and Britany works at a hunting lodge. She's pregnant now too.

TEDDY

Teddy lives with his fifth set of foster parents. He's in a special education 6:1:1 program, receives psychiatric counseling, and has his own aide for a prior molestation incident with a small foster sibling. He is thirteen years old, very tall and heavyset and awkward. His pants ride high above his waist, and he smells of body odor. He can be very friendly and respectful (the Eddie Haskel act), but he is subject to rage outbursts. Like so many of these students, he dutifully reports to the nurse each day for doses of Adderall, Abilify, and Ativan. Rudy and JT are called to Fletcher's room one afternoon, where Teddy has thrown a desk and refuses to leave the room. Rudy and JT position themselves on either side of him as he shouts threats and curses, and in seconds, he is on the floor in full restraint. JT looks almost relaxed with his own legs stretched out and crossed alongside Teddy's body while holding his arm pinned behind his back. Rudy is on the other side, waiting for him to tire and wiping the mucus from his nasal passages as he continues to try to kick his legs and rage hysterically. His social worker contacts the foster mother, who says Teddy is grounded for stealing cookies that she hid for her own children, and she "told" Teddy they were not for him.

I have visions of Teddy killing his foster parents with a kitchen knife—their mutilated bodies bleeding on the floor at his feet while he sits and eats a big sandwich. I recommend placement at a 24-7 facility that will cost the district $87,000 per year, but I know if he stays with us, he is a ticking time bomb.

JUDY JACZNEWSKI

There are a few rules at school that are always a source of annual administrator-teacher conflict and show up on the "school team improvement" meeting agendas ad nauseam. Students are expected to remove their hats when they enter the building, and for most of them, it is a pretty automatic gesture as they come in the bus doors. For others, it is always some sort of a "test" to see if anyone will say anything to them or signal that something is up and they need to talk. The origin of the rule goes back to an incident before I was there, when a student entered the cafeteria with a box cutter hidden in the rim of the baseball cap and slashed another student. When cell phones became popular, that too became a zero-tolerance rule, the rationale being that it could potentially be a security issue with kids communicating with individuals outside the school and arranging clandestine drug deals and/or staging plans to fight. The biggest complaint from teachers is that there is "no consistency," and the brunt of enforcement resides with the principal and AP. I never had difficulty just looking at a student, to have them immediately remove the hat, put the cell phone away, and even add "Oh, sorry, Miz R., I forgot." It also gave me and them an excuse to interact—ask how things were going, see if they had eaten, inquire about the recent English test, or comment on the great art project they did. Lenny and the Kid didn't have any trouble either, but as the staff would say, "Well, *you* all have the power!" (So did Evie, Evan, Rudy, JT, the great Spellini, and many other teachers in the building who spent time at the beginning of each year, for as long as it took, to build a community of respect in their classrooms and agree on certain nonnegotiable rules for conduct.) I was particularly fond of Gloria, the teaching assistant, who was posted on hall duty as the students entered the building. Every morning, they walked by her, greeted by her nonsmiling face, brows knitted together—which made for an unmistakenly ugly scowl—and her arms intertwined across her chest. Inevitably, she would later grace my doorway, this time with a sickening smile pasted across her face, and say, "Excuse me, Mrs. Robbin, but did I *miss* something? Do we *now* allow hats or skirts so short, they reveal *under*wear? Or didn't *you* notice how low Lizzie's blouse was?" Never once did she address the issue with the student, so we just called her the informant.

But Judy Jacznewski, by far, won the prize for not only not enforcing the rules, but crossing every boundary a teacher can cross with students, especially those adept at manipulating adults as soon as they detect the slightest vulnerability. Judy is a very popular teacher at the alternative school. Students know they can wear hats without her giving them trouble and come late to her class. They know they can use cell phones in her room, and why shouldn't they when Judy spends half her time behind her desk, texting her boyfriend? They also know Judy's boyfriend (a former alt student), with a rap sheet as long as the Mississippi River (according to Deputy Dole). Judy, or Jaz, as she is known by the students—and since she encourages the nickname by using it to sign passes for kids or even notes to me—wants students to know she is their "friend." She has a Facebook page and writes to them, has their phone numbers logged into her cell phone, and as a protest against the Obama election when the inauguration was being shown on a wide screen in the library (since she thought that meant the school was endorsing Obama), she convinced a group of her boys, who sported confederate flag logos on their hats, to skip school, and she took them to the mall.

In January, even a hint of snow can create early closings, delayed openings, or school cancellations. In my school experience as a student, I rarely remember a snow day. If it snowed, the bus driver would pull over, put chains on the tires, and we would continue to school or home, wherever the destination. One afternoon, when there was an early closing and I was still at school, I received a frantic call from Judy, who had left shortly after the buses. She had been in an accident and totaled her car. I asked if she was OK and told her to just "take it easy," and we would see her when she was "better." Judy sustained whiplash and was out for four months on paid sick leave. Although there were Jaz sightings at the mall and her students managed to visit her regularly, Judy sent in doctors' notes and occasionally checked in with the school to update us on her return. Her classes were out of control. The substitute, who was duly certified to teach science, complained students did not seem to be used to work or even know the most basic material. On one of the real snow days, when I was in—as administrators did not get snow days—I went to Judy's room, which was a disaster. In the floor-to-ceiling closets, there were opened containers of every kind of glitter and dried-up tubes of glue. There was a bookcase crammed with torn-out pages of magazines, stacks and stacks of them. There were computers in the back of the room missing cords and keyboards. Her desk had piles of paper, some of which appeared to be students' half-completed work, some which resembled half-done acrostic puzzles. Under her desk, I found two broken microscopes; and in the desk drawers were scissors, Kleenex, cough drops, nail polish, and gum. I ordered a Dumpster and began to purge Judy's room of trash and rearrange the furniture.

I kept Alexis updated on all of Judy's infractions, and her response was always "Write her up!" My file on Judy was now so thick, and I had met with her numerous times. At first, it was a series of nonthreatening, informal discussions that appealed to her sense of professionalism as a teacher. I even spent a faculty meeting on the subject of "boundaries" with students so it didn't look as though Judy was being singled out. With the condition of the room, I knew the cell phone lines would be lit up, as Judy's moles reported back to her. Judy returned to school the next Monday. She had now three memos in her mailbox regarding the condition of her room, the lack of lesson plans provided while she was out, and the school equipment found destroyed in her room. We were to meet and discuss the memos the afternoon of her return. She entered my office with the rep who, as usual, wore her Cheshire cat grin. Judy never showed any affect as she vehemently denied all of the allegations. Rep defended her as "an excellent science teacher" who had the misfortune of having an accident and was being unduly reprimanded.

As Judy and the rep left my office, Judy turned back to me and said, "I hope you didn't throw away all the magazines since the students use them for collages, and they were my own *personal* property." Judy is a tenured teacher, six years with the school. Her track record, as far as student performance on the Regents is concerned, is negligible, and I understand the reason she is not allowed to grade exams is that she was suspected of changing answers by a colleague, which went unproven.

I am directed, from Rhoda via Alexis, to put her on an improvement plan. Rhoda stops in one day and tells me, "You can make her a better teacher." I actually have to meet with this useless excuse for a teacher once a week and go over her lesson plans. Within weeks, a student shows a cell phone video to a teacher of Judy in her classroom being twirled around on her desk chair with wheels, groped at by the boys in the class as she spins, and the sound is of Judy laughing and saying, "Stoppp it, you guys . . . stoppp it." It is further reported by one of Judy's "friends" that she told the students she was "sooo sore from all the fucking she did while she was out."

I go back to Alexis, and we obtain a copy of the cell phone video, which she passes along to Rhoda and Buddy. He wants us to bring in the students to question them. I refuse to allow the students to be brought into the situation and recommend that Judy be terminated immediately. Buddy directs Alexis to interview Judy, with me present, and show her the film. Judy arrives at Alexis's office with the rep and me. Upon seeing herself, hearing herself, seeing her room, the kids, the spinning chair, her reply is "I don't think that's me. I don't have a sweater that color." *(Right . . . and nobody else in the building has orange spiked hair).*

We wait a week. A parent calls Alexis and asks to meet with her about one of the teachers. Alexis asks me to come to the meeting. Mrs. X enters the office in tight leggings, low-cut scooped-neck sweater, high-heel boots, and a faux fur coat. She tells us she doesn't want Jaz to know she is there, but she is worried about some things that the kids are telling her. Apparently, Frankie, Jaz's boyfriend, comes to Mrs. X's house to hang out with her son and his friends, some of whom go to our school. She said she has heard Frankie, sitting at her own kitchen table, call Jaz "a bitch who only gives him $75 a week" to watch her kid. She tells us he has "threatened to kill the boys if they ever rat him out for saying any of this." Mrs. X then pulls out the last stop and tells us she too has had a brief affair with Frankie, but it is over. She is really just worried that the boys are "afraid" of him. Mrs. X does not want to be identified and asks that we get her escorted out of the building so there is no chance Jaz sees her.

Alexis and I are stunned. This is like a third-rate movie, only there is no doubt in my mind it is all true. Alexis brings it back to Rhoda and Buddy, whose position is that we don't "have enough" evidence to terminate, and I am to continue with my improvement plan meetings with Judy.

I write "just the facts" in a memo and recommend immediate termination for Judy so my position is clearly on file. Judy is sharing information with the students about how we are out to get her, and students are letting out information in defense of Judy, which unnerves me. They are clearly caught in the middle of an adult war that is out of control. In tandem with this is a married teacher's aide who is confiding in a student about her unhappy sex life. She is reprimanded, and the parent of the student comes in to complain that this aide texts her son constantly. They refuse to expose the aide for fear of "invading" their son's privacy. They want him to graduate, but they will not hesitate to "go to the press" if we don't do something about the aide. Their son is also suspected of dealing drugs provided by Frankie. The aide is written up, denies all the allegations, and reports back to the student. I feel like we are sitting on a powder keg. The rep is fueling the fire by talking to Rhoda.

Rhoda, once again, stops by my office unannounced, and I tell her the boundary issues with these two staff members are beyond repair and having a disastrous, almost snowballing effect on the students. She tells me to "back the fuck off."

Deputy Dole is late one morning several weeks later. He answered a a call in the middle of the night on one of our students. He was at a party and overdosed. He is dead. For the rest of the year, we manage the "grievance process" for students who cannot begin to understand the scope of this tragedy. I allow them to put a memorial service together for their lost friend and invite his family. Students get up and tearfully read poems or tell stories about him. A few teachers get up and talk about some of the funny things he used to do in class. I hold my breath when Judy gets up and walks to the microphone. She starts to speak but breaks down in tears. One of the girls gets out of the bleachers and goes to comfort her. Judy leans on her shoulder, sobbing loudly as they walk back to their seats.

Chapter Sixteen

Unions have no place in the educational profession. They have served to systemize and legitimize individuals who quite simply are lazy, stupid, and/ or mentally unbalanced. If the intent was to prevent whimsical, unfair, without-due-process treatment from administrators, they failed miserably, minimally, at the expense of the taxpayer, but even more so in the irreparable damage to the educational fabric of our children's lives. The union voice is not the voice of the best teacher—it is just the loudest voice.

RUDY

His very presence is a crackling, staccato beat—*pop, pop, pop*—continuous rounds of automatic ammunition, relentless in their force and energy. His vision is hawklike, surveying the entire landscape in one sweep—knowing exactly where to choose the ripe prey. Many are fooled at first—just a crisis worker trained in "restraint," force enough to take down a surly adolescent and render him weak and whining, exposing the raw core of vulnerability. The voice, heavily Hispanic, not quite fluid, not smoothed out, but rough—without pretense. He's deferential, sometimes walking as one who recognizes his place; following a master, slightly shrinking his 5'5" size, and in a split second, can rise to the stature of a giant; omnipotent, with the strength to take out an army and the tenderness to melt diamonds. His senses are acute, honed to invincibility-bionic. He could kill as expertly and efficiently as he could break your heart with his kindness. He is a superhuman—not from this planet, a gift to this earth, and the single most important inspiration to educators and the very best reason to hope for students.

Rudy works three jobs. He arrives at the alternative school and leaves as soon as buses depart at 2:45 PM. He then drives ten miles to a residential school for younger boys, where he does after-school recreational activities—planting, cooking, and harvesting vegetables. On Friday and Saturday nights, he travels between local and regional gigs with his own band. He's the lead singer, drummer, tour manager, booking agent, producer, and publicist. The love of his life is his nine-year-old daughter who's smart, beautiful, talented, generous, and "of another world" like her dad.

Rudy's gaze penetrates the soul. He masks this extraordinary power with effusive, self-effacing humor and enthusiasm. He's ahead of every interaction—way beyond the opening dialogue; he's at the middle and at the end and has moved on. Nothing perplexes him, arrests him in his tracks, intimidates or surprises him. He relishes the process of seeing each student, teacher, and staff person search for the right passage through the maze—Rudy is always waiting patiently at the end. I've seen Rudy take the biggest and most hard-core delinquent and hypnotize them with his voice. He endears, cajoles, imitates, becomes their thoughts vocalized (accents and gestures included), then shocks and commands them to a better place. He strips the veneer—layer by layer—angling to penetrate their hardened cores. Rudy can get the gun—always, without fail.

Alexis bought us all new appliances the second year, and we dedicated an entire room to the kitchen. Rudy called it the "multipurpose" room as he was never in there with students for just the purpose of cooking. As a brother to ten siblings and a master chef, Rudy knew his way around a kitchen, grocery store, and steel sharpened knives in his sleep. The year we offered electives, Rudy's ninth-period cooking was neck and neck with Willy's film. Alexis allocated about $150 a month (nowhere near enough to feed a population of 170 students on free and reduced lunch, but Rudy made it stretch), and students sought out Rudy all day long. In the winter, he brought in a chicken carcass from Sunday night dinner and had a big pot of soup going by 10:00 AM Monday morning. As the sights, aroma of exotic spices, and sounds of the kitchen wafted through the halls, white lightning chili; braised venison; split pea soup with ham hocks, rice, and beans; and paella became common fare.

A student arriving late, cold and hungry, would shift from foot to foot, silent, not quite ready to go to class, when a "Come on, pappy, you need some breakfast, I'll scramble you up some eggs" uttered from Rudy would instantly change the mood and, in almost every case, change the course of the day for the student.

Alternative kids don't tell you they're hungry. They treat the cafeteria like sacred space. At Woodland Valley, students would leave trays filled with untouched food, unopened cartons of milk thrown later in the trash bins. At alternative, students ate every crumb of cardboard pizza, every slightly stale bagel spread with a meager portion of cream cheese doled out in a tiny plastic cup. They drank their milk, ate government-issued cheese, and emptied their own trash.

Once, I found a sullen student outside my office during his lunch period. "What's wrong? Did you have lunch?"

"No . . . they won't give it to me."

"Why not?"

"They say my paperwork isn't signed yet."

I go to the cafeteria with a personal check for fifty dollars made out to the "school lunch fund" and hand it to Nadine. "No student is to ever be turned down for breakfast or lunch. Keep this as my tab and let me know when it runs out." Nadine's eyes widen as she sees the amount. I get e-mails when the fund is running low.

Rudy's cooking class is capped at nineteen; no one is ever out of area or late. They write up shopping lists, make budgets, measure, sift, pour, braise, bake, simmer, and stir their way in interdisciplinary activity. They scrub, shave, garnish, and grate. Plant herbs and sample spices—they're alive with learning. His radio crackles constantly. "Ru, your location? Go to room 207 to remove a student," "Rudy—check out Haller's room!" "Rudy, crisis in REO!" Rudy, Rudy, Rudy.

Teachers begin to complain that they are not being supported—Rudy is "rewarding" kids who have missed their classes (well, they didn't miss Rudy's class). Rudy is "never" around in the halls when they need him (what, because you can't take a cell phone away from them?). Rudy is counterproductive to their efforts.

Rudy runs around the kitchen at lightning speed—reading eyes, engaging kids, developing bonds, counseling, laughing, guiding, advising, persuading, changing lives . . . and teaching.

Toxic rep gets to Rhoda again. I am asked to attend a meeting with the doctor. "Well, what's different—what's the progress at the alternative school, and don't tell me it's about Rudy and the cooking."

I snap back, "It's *all* about Rudy and the cooking!"

As the weather warms, Rudy is given fifty dollars for planting and grounds keeping. Within weeks, the once stark campus has been dug up, replanted, trimmed, and mulched and flowers bloom in surprise bunches. The entryway, once full of unfriendly, stalky, shaved-off bushes, are blooming with day lilies, tulips, and hydrangea. Rudy's crew includes some of the most disturbed, potentially violent, oppositional, defiant ADD kids we have. He commands them like young soldiers—gives them extra responsibility to maintain tools, water plants, and unload mulch deliveries. They ask for ways to earn "special" time to work "grounds." Again, I field the complaints.

"Jordan was working with Rudy and not in my class."

"But you kicked him *out* of your class."

"Well, Rudy is re*warding* him, and administrators are *allowing* it to happen!"

I tell her, "He counsels, he supports you, he's trying to 'ready' them for the discipline of the classroom."

"Counseling? Well, I'm not so sure. If I needed counseling, I'd go to a crisis worker."

(Reallllly. I would refer them to their social worker, but she hid behind my door when he punched a wall and didn't want to talk to him. Hmmm . . . if you are a social worker, afraid of adolescent anger, why are you here? We have four of them, times $65,000 per year plus benefits.)

Rudy fulfills a life dream and buys his first house. It is a huge old Victorian with sixteen rooms and a dual-heating system—one oil and one wood fueled. He has yet another job to add to his routine: finding, chopping and feeding the furnace he calls the beast. He chops and feeds all throughout the brutally cold winter and says, "I love it, Ms. R!" He hosts thirty-five friends and family for Thanksgiving, and most of them stay over. His elderly parents attend. His mother still works for a family in Manhattan. His father is in a wheelchair. Rudy constructs a special lift to bring him up the outside stairs where he will be able to wheel himself around the main floor. With a glass of something special on the kitchen counter, he banters with his mother while they cook. Rudy doesn't complain—ever. One day, he will just disappear, probably to return to his own planet, his work here on earth completed, his words echoing in my ears: "It's all about the love, Ms. R."

WINSTON

Winston is a seventeen-year-old African American referred from a large urban district. He is prohibited from being on their property. He is tall, handsome, and smart and walks with a cocky gait. Winston lives with his grandmother and two younger sisters. He has a full academic schedule, but the work is easy for him, so he spends a lot of time socializing with the girls, hanging out in the gym, and just being "Mr. Cool." Evie and Rudy have a good relationship with him. Evie talks to his grandmother, who is worried that Winston is out late on weekends, and she is afraid of what he might be getting into. Rudy sits him down in my office. Winston has a red do-rag hanging from his back pocket.

"What's up, Win?" Rudy asks.

"What you mean, Ru?" Winston replies straight-faced.

"Don't dis me man, what's with the bullshit red rag? Why you bringin' this shit into my school?"

Rudy's voice is cutting and sharp and gets Winston's attention.

"Nothin', Ru, just some guys I see. I'm not in any gang stuff, I know what I'm doin'."

A few days later, Winston comes in wearing an expensive pair of sneakers, too expensive for his grandmother to afford. Rudy yanks him aside again, only this time, Winston is more arrogant.

"Let it go, Ru! I'm not doin' anything."

"You're headed down a bad road, man. They'll use you and spit you out when they're done."

Winston backs off a little. He knows Rudy is just worried about him. Winston is slick. He moves in and out of small groups of kids, abruptly breaks up discussions when he sees JT or Rudy. Fridays are active drug-trading days. It's the weekend, and there are innocent yellow buses that unknowingly facilitate transport over a 550-square mile radius.

On Monday, Winston is absent. His grandmother calls Evie and says he has been arrested at three in the morning on Sunday, standing on a street corner with three hundred bags of crack. Winston is in jail. A few weeks later, Evie and Rudy decide to visit him at the correctional facility before school. Rudy tells Evie not to wear any jewelry or bring anything, that they will be searched before going in. After getting through security, they are led into a room with a bank of plexiglass cubicles where inmates sit on one side and the visitor sits opposite them, and they speak through a round "talk" disk in the center. Winston doesn't know they are coming, so when he is led in by a guard, he scans the visitors to see who is there to see him. He is in an orange jumpsuit, hands cuffed in front of him, and is guided to a chair by the guard. "Ten minutes" is all the guard says. Evie stays velcroed to Rudy, having already suffered the stares and catcalls of the inmates as they walked in. Despite her attempts at looking plain, without the eye makeup and gloss, her youth and beauty radiate through the dull space. As soon as Winston sees them, he drops his head to his chest.

Rudy starts right in. "I'm pissed, man. I'm really angry with you, Win. What were you *thinking*? I *told* you they were makin' you . . . for *what*? A $500 pair of *fuckin' sneakers*!"

Winston does not look at them but is silent, his head still hung down on his chest. He answers no questions, gives no sign that he is even listening.

"Three minutes," the guard calls out from the door.

Finally, Winston says, "Will I be able to come back to school?"

"Welllll, I don't know about *that*!" Rudy replies. "That's up to Miz Ro. If I were you, I'd write her a letter if you are so *interested* in going back to school. Right now, you're looking at four months. You got a lot to *think* about."

A week later, I receive a letter from Winston, a full page of apologies and remorse, telling me he promises he will "turn it around" if only he can have a chance to come back and graduate. Evie cries as she reads it. She has invested so much time in him and his family—brought food to their house, prepped him for exams, and made sure he did his work. I write him back, opening my letter with correcting his spelling on some of his words to knock him down a few more notches, but I end with promising him there will always be a place for him at the school when he gets out. Winston serves his time and refuses a shortened sentence in return for turning in the "big dealer." He has already been threatened, if he snitches, with the life of his grandmother.

Winston returns four months later, and we have already begun the school year. He has catching up to do, but he is a model student. He is looked upon by the other students as some kind of a hero. They don't mess with him. He spends any free time cooking in the kitchen with Rudy, talking. That's the bond that enables him to talk about what happened. In March, Winston is nominated as Most Outstanding Senior, and along with two others who win high academic achievement status, he and his grandmother are invited to a countywide dinner with other similar students at the Primrose Country Club.

All the principals and superintendents attend and are usually seated at tables with the students from their districts. I arrive after the "social" hour and find there is no place card for me outside the dining room. Buddy is MC for the event and tells me he is sure there is one for me. I tell him not to worry; I will find a seat at a table after I say hello to our students and their families. As I enter the dining room, there are at least fifteen tables for ten placed around the room. All the tables are full with laughing, talking guests, except for one that is dead center in the room where Winston and his grandmother and an uncle are seated alone. They are the only African American people in the room. I am stunned at this blatant, insensitive seating arrangement. I see Dr. Rhoda sitting a few tables away with board members. I walk over to Winston's table. He is wearing a new green dress shirt and tie with black pants. His grandmother is wearing a flowery dress, and his uncle has a semiwrinkled white shirt with a tie. I hug Grandma and Winston and introduce myself to the uncle.

Winston says, "I hope you're at our table, Miz R."

"Well, I sure am, and I wouldn't sit anyplace else!"

I then tell Grandma how proud we are of Winston and have a discussion with the uncle about his small business that is suffering the effects of a dying economy. Winston gets his award, a fifty-dollar check, after listening to the main speaker talk about his own business in the community. Sitting in this room of regional school administrators, students, parents, and local business leaders, in this country club decorated in beige brocade, being served chicken and green beans and some version of chocolate pudding for dessert, I am deeply ashamed at how short this display of "recognition" for achieving students falls.

CHAPTER SEVENTEEN

At an assembly when I introduced Lenny and the Kid to the students and staff, students spontaneously whistled and cheered and welcomed them both with overwhelming enthusiasm. The fact that they had an administrator "of color" and a young (the Kid is thirty-two) and very hip intern brought a freshness and credibility to the perverse reign of Gordon. Each morning, we gathered in my office and mapped out new strategies for change. The punitive model was defunct, and we began to "push back," asking teachers what they were doing exactly to keep the students in class and engaged in learning. The great Spellini was making inroads with the "mountain kids" who deliberately kept brandishing their confederate flag belt buckles and T-shirts. The small-group mediations and student-teacher sessions refereed by one of us or Evie or Evan or Rudy were commonplace. Students were finding their voice and feeling more responsibility for the creation and maintenance of their culture. We set up case management meetings, identifying "red flag" students, and came together in small groups to discuss individual students and examine all the factors affecting their behaviors. The scales seemed to be tipping, and the first to pick up on this monumental shift were the students. More and more walked into my office to express their dissatisfaction: "I want out of that class." "I can't learn." "I'm bored. All we do is watch movies."

One morning the Kid found a student in the hall and asked why he wasn't in class.

"She kicked me out 'cause I was late."

"OK, well, let's go get the work you missed."

112

The Kid arrives at the door, and the teacher says, "He was twenty minutes late."

The Kid says, "What did he miss?"

The teacher says, "Uhh, nothing, we haven't really started yet."

The Kid says, "Well, then I guess he is not late."

And the student was admitted to class. Teachers resort to new tactics as the squeeze is applied to keep students engaged. They push buttons and know exactly how to do it to provoke a chair shoved, a book thrown, or an expletive shouted. Teachers use the term "violence, staff assault, verbal abuse—how much are we supposed to take?" They say, "This is an unsafe environment." Meanwhile, our VADIR (state report on incidents of violence) score is sooooo low; there has been no violence, few fights, and no instances of weapons in the building. Lenny is quickly tiring of the whiny nature of the staff and is on his cell phone placing feelers out for new positions. After Thanksgiving break, our discussion turns to an "academy" structure—a junior academy for the ninth and tenth grade and a senior academy for the juniors and seniors. By January, we share these ideas with the staff and tell them they will help create this team structure. Union rep is now in her element, threatening to grieve the issue, stating special education law, and—it's for sure—yet another filtered idea is going to the coffeehouse.

Lenny, the Kid, and I share the plan with Alexis. She tells us to write a proposal and submit it to her, and she will format it in final form. The three of us work over winter break and divide the proposal into three sections. I take the historical, overview, and vision section; the Kid takes the curricular structure; and Lenny includes a work study program so important for the older adolescents. We put the three sections together in three different typed formats. The Kid checks prices at Staples for reformatting and color printing, which are exorbitant. Alexis says she will "take care of it." Alexis informs us that we will all meet with Buddy and Dr. Rhoda in a week to discuss the proposal.

We enter Alexis's office, and Alexis is at one head of the conference table. Buddy and Dr. Rhoda are seated side by side, and Lenny takes a seat at the opposite head from Alexis. The Kid and I sit on the side, me opposite Dr. Rhoda and the Kid opposite Buddy. No one is smiling but the three of us. There is palpable tension: Alexis is wide-eyed and expectant. Dr. Rhoda is looking down into her lap. Lenny sits back with his hands folded across his stomach, surveying each player as he would from the sidelines of his basketball games when he was honored as Coach of the Year. The kid sits straight up with a smile, and I am blissfully oblivious to these body postures and expressions and predispositions already painted on this canvas.

I begin with the overview—where we are, what we have achieved, and where we would like to go. I cite our good data and our weak spots. I describe in detail the changing population of referrals and our need to continue a redesign of alternative. The Kid jumps in a few times, giving relevant examples from his experience at a charter school in Brooklyn. Alexis's eyes dart from the speaker to the superintendent, almost as though she is waiting to speak before declaring her allegiance, which must be to the winning team. Rhoda's head is bowed so low, it is almost on the table. Lenny has already sensed what is about to come. Buddy's face is ashen. When I finish, his first words uttered are, "The *fonts*! You didn't even use the same fonts, and it looks like all three of you prepared different sections." Lenny looks immediately to Alexis. "Yes," I reply, "we did talk about making it pretty. This is a draft." I'm smiling, thinking this is a joke first comment. He's kidding with us, and I see Lenny's face and, in the back of my mind, remember Alexis was supposed to "make it pretty" and finalize the draft. Alexis is silent. Rhoda is stonelike. Lenny doesn't move. The kid just stares at Buddy, and I finally react viscerally to the punch. Buddy continues his rant. "If this were a dissertation, you'd all get a D!" He proceeds page by page, citing fonts, outdated quotes from educational theorists, and typos. Not once does he address pedagogy, not once does he respond to the compelling data, the revenues, the population shifts in intakes, and the inefficiency and expense of the current model. Not once does he respond to or even contribute to a vision for the program. "This is a *school*—we are here to graduate kids—we're not a therapeutic center." And with that last statement, I know that 1) Rhoda's head indicates she has already prepped him from the information received at her weekly chatter with toxic rep; 2) Alexis has distanced herself from us and set us up rather than doing her part, and my mind does flips like a snapping camera shutter to what must have been hundreds of cabinet meetings where her position was clearly always on the home team (of course, how else to survive on the bully's turf); and 3) that for me, the work is done. What I thought I was hired for was not in fact the case. Change—too rapid, too honest, too logical, too bright—although astoundingly good for kids, threatens the nerve center of the adults in power.

I know as I thank them for their time and pack up my books, articles, yellow highlighter, and data, it is over. And I see with astonishing clarity my three years of work and, with laser-like precision, their responses—each step, each incident. The pieces fall into place, rattling like the metal funnel on the coin machine at the bank, each separate metal denomination falling precisely into its designated tube—everything fits, just as it was intended. I am so calm; I take the thick "academy" folder and put it with my basket of things to go home. We will not be doing a new version or a cleaned-up model as suggested; we won't be going for the A plus, and as Matt Damon said in *Good Will Hunting*, "How do ya like them apples?" Alexis later comes to my office where Lenny, the Kid, and I are replaying the meeting, and the Kid has us both hysterically laughing. "Please don't hate me for throwing you under the bus," she blurts, somewhat relieved we are all laughing.

Lenny lands a job as an AP at an inner city high school for more money and leaves in the fall. The Kid lands a job as an AP at a regional middle school but turns it down on the hope he will get Lenny's position. When all is said and done, the Kid and I partner up by October of the new school year so I can give him a few more pointers before I pack it in. Buddy abruptly retires. It's only a brief paragraph on the second page of the paper.

If it is a weekday, one of the 180 days a year required for the school calendar, yellow buses will roll, kids will enter school buildings, and teachers, principals, and support staff will be present to do the work called "education." Some will be exceptionally talented, hardworking, prepared, engaging, humorous, and empathetic. Others will be lazy, unprepared, alienating, punitive, and self-serving.

KALUB

We are getting a new student for our life skills program. He is seventeen and a half and new to this country from Budapest. His father tells the district he is "very limited" and likes to work with animals and hopes we will be able to give him some basic skills so he can work. Life skills students study basic math (making change and understanding monetary denominations), basic social skills, and language skills and spend half a day at the career center learning to wash and prep vegetables and stock ingredient shelves. The expectation is that they will go on to work in a supervised setting or sheltered workshop.

Kalub arrives by bus and comes to the entrance where I am there to greet him. He is easily six feet tall, thin, and wears wide-rail corduroys and a thin shirt. His long hair is parted in the middle and falls below his waist, and there is a slight trace of a mustache. His head is down, and he isn't carrying anything. "Welcome," I say enthusiastically. Kalub nods his head. I tell him I will bring him to his class right down the hall. Kalub enters the room and sits at a vacant desk in the front with his hands folded in front of him. Each day is the same routine. He gets off the bus with the same clothes on, does not speak as we greet him, and goes promptly to his class. On my way home, I see Kalub walking down Route 222—sometimes with an older man I presume to be his father, sometimes alone.

A few weeks later, Evie comes to my office and asks if I can see Kalub. She says he came to her office and just started sobbing. Kalub sits in a chair with Evie and me on either side of him. We take turns gently asking him what is wrong—is it the school, his classes, another student, his home? We wait with him at least twenty minutes before he speaks (Evie and I trade looks about what could possibly be going on).

"Zey saaay America izt goot land . . . but I donsz find izt zo goot. Budapest izt better . . ."

(Now we're getting somewhere.)

Evie jumps in. "Kalub, why is Budapest better? Did you have friends?"

"Ya . . . I haf friends, and my mozur is dere . . . but . . . my fazur think izt better in America . . ."

Evie says, "Kalub, you can do *anything* you want to do in America, but it is hard to move here from another country. Give it a little time."

Typical of Rudy, who has been doing the rounds in the building, he peeks through the office glass window and sees us talking, and I motion him in. He already knows Kalub and greets him with, "Hey, pappy, what's goin' on?" Kalub actually gives him a smile. I tell Rudy we have just been talking about how much Kalub misses Budapest. Rudy, already with a grip on the whole scene—including Kalub's swollen eyes—goes into a story about coming to this country from Columbia with his ten brothers and sisters and sitting in a classroom where he did not know one word of English. He has Kalub laughing in no time. Evie and I are thinking the exact same thing: why is this kid in a life skills program?

Eventually, since Kalub labors with his speech and is very deliberate in the choice of his limited words, I promise Kalub he will never go back to the life skills class, he will have a totally different schedule, and we will handpick his classes. Kalub tells us he lives in one room with his father, and they have to share the same bed. So he walks around town every day. "I juss walk and walk . . . I doan mind." We put him in Fisher's creative nonfiction class, and Fisher discovers he is interested in acting. He and another student partner up to write a play. We put him in Spellini's history class and tell Spellini Kalub could share his experiences about life in Budapest. Kalub likes to work on the computer, so we give him a period with Charlene in the library, and of course, Rudy tells him he must come to cooking and they will create some good ole-fashioned Hungarian dishes.

Kalub also tells us he has a plan. "When I am atezteen [eighteen], I am going to get my pazzport from my fazur, and I am going back to Budapest. He hidez it from me."

Evie pipes up, "Oh, we will help you get your passport, Kalub, if you want to go home."

Kalub's birthday is in March.

All through the winter months, Kalub follows his individual schedule, and Chantel befriends him along with several other girls who think he's "cute." I continue to see him walking in all kinds of weather after school hours. Just before his birthday, he comes smiling to my office with Maxine, who asks if he needs permission to have his hair cut over in the cosmetology lab. "Well," I reply, "he is going to be eighteen, so I suspect Kalub is man enough to make his own decision about getting his hair cut." His father has been a persistent caller and e-mailer to the district school and to us, complaining that Kalub still does not have some kind of training in taking care of animals. Since Kalub has already told us, "Welll . . . I like animalz . . . but . . . you know . . . they can hurtz you too." He has shown more interest in playwriting, which his father totally dismisses as "absurd."

Kalub comes back from cosmo with his hair cut to shoulder-length and a big smile on his face. The girls are in awe, squealing that he "looks just like Johnny Depp!" which he does. He tells me he never thought he could feel so "lighter" and so "happy."

Kalub has never missed a day of school, but after his eighteenth birthday, he no longer comes. We find out from his father, he has left home and gone to live with a "former" friend of the father's. Eventually, Kalub is withdrawn from the program by the district due to lack of attendance.

Somewhere in the beautiful city of Budapest, I hope a brilliant young Johnny Depp look-alike is making his way in an acting career.

EPILOGUE

In September of my last year, Lenny is already in exit mode to begin his new job on October 1. The Kid can come on board as assistant principal, although he still has to endure the interviews of shared decision making before an official appointment. The students circulate a petition protesting Lenny's departure and give it to him with all their signatures as a parting gift, but knowing the Kid will be replacing him seems to keep them in good spirits and looking forward to the year. Lenny continues to pitch the Kid and me on starting our own school and places calls regularly to investors who might support it.

It is a Wednesday afternoon, and Alexis cancels our weekly supervisors' meeting. The forecast calls for a nor'easter bringing heavy rain and high winds. I wheel my cart up and down the aisles with ease and actually check out without a line. Packed up and ready to leave the parking lot, I notice black rolling clouds over the mountains in the distance and the sky is darkening. The day was perfect—the kids were in sync, and there were few staff absences. No crises to untangle and no suspensions, but it is still early in the year. The last few miles home, torrential rain is falling. My windshield wipers are on "fast" speed and can barely handle the leaves being stripped from the trees by the unrelenting wind gusts. There is already a roadblock for a fallen power line on Route 222, so I detour to the steeper side of the mountain. Thunder, lightning and hail pound the car as I slowly navigate the turns up the steep grade. Less than half a mile from my home, I hear a large bang, and everything goes black.

"We've already called it in, hon, the ambulance is on the way."

"No, don't move her."

My eyes are closed, but I hear the words of a woman and man shouting over the sound of wind and snapping branches. As I open my eyes, I see smoke to my right and think the car is going to blow up. I feel for the door handle, and a very tall fireman opens it from the other side and helps me out.

A tree has smashed diagonally across my car deploying the passenger side airbag.

I am out of school for the next two days to do the emergency room checkup and arrange a rental car. I am back in school to greet buses by Monday morning. I am determined to be as normal as possible since my absence can trigger staff absences. Except for the fact that a rental Honda is parked in the space usually inhabited by my Audi, not many people notice, and I am met with the same number of people in line, waiting to relate their issues of the day when I arrive at the office.

"Oh, sorry about your accident, but Evan changed a schedule, and I am one over in students because there should only be six, and now there are seven."

"Yes, but so 'n' so is being withdrawn soon, so really, you don't have seven bodies in the class."

"I know, but still, it's a very rowdy class, and DaShawn is very disruptive. I mean, I don't want to cause trouble or anything, but see what you can do."

The Kid brings a level of energy and enthusiasm and wit and humor that is invigorating. He literally runs around the building, problem solving and shaking cobwebs out of the mindsets of the veteran teachers. Rep retired the past June, but a duo of her followers quickly step into her shoes. The

Kid is irreverent in his treatment of them. When he pairs up with Rudy or JT, I am left holding my sides together from laughing so hard. The Kid is thin as a rail but eats like a wrestler. Rudy says, "It's time to feed the beast!" And the Kid shows up along with the regular kids when the kitchen is generating a salsa beat. Alexis tells Rudy she can no longer fund the kitchen food budget, and we are headed for big cutbacks. I give him a check for three hundred dollars to get in some basics, and Rudy says he will stretch it until January.

At faculty meetings, I am uncertain as to where we are going. I tell the staff the comment was made that there was no staff buy-in for the academy proposal and ask them what they would like to focus on for the year. They have no clue, except that status quo is just fine with them. I point out we will suffer in enrollment unless we offer some different approaches for alternative kids and that we are now getting a more dangerous population that will not respond to traditional methodology. The Kid decides to initiate "early morning quick meetings" twice a week, which start at 8:00 AM and last fifteen minutes to force them to collaborate. He reinstitutes the sign-in sheet so when they shuffle in, the most important thing is to get their name on the sheet. He tells them he would like lesson plan overviews turned in every two weeks. Some he receives, some he doesn't, and the union explores grieving his right to ask for them. He sends notices for the ones he doesn't get, which go ignored, and Alexis tells him she is "powerless" to make them do them. By December, the Kid has established his place as an administrator, and I take a backseat to his initiatives, feeling more and more like it is time to pass the torch. The Kid has yet to experience the politics of central office and the disingenuous methods of Dr. Rhoda, who has been left to make the decisions since Buddy's departure. He is hopeful and energetic and ready to take on the program for yet another attempt at moving it forward.

I tell Alexis that I am considering retirement and will give my notice the first of April. She tears up, and we spend a few moments worrying about how we will swap fashion magazines. I tell the Kid I will teach him all there is to know since he is the best candidate to continue with such a dysfunctional group. I know he is on a career ladder that he will quickly climb. The kid is so brilliant, but he will know when it is time to cut his losses with the program.

We have an unusually flawless graduation. A former student, now attending college, comes back as a guest speaker. The mood is upbeat, the parents are proud, and the entire school celebrates the day. Despite my admonitions that there are to be no parties for me, the Kid arranges a surprise gathering of the entire school in the cafeteria with a cake and a few student speakers who present me with a beautiful card, framed photograph of their outdoor organic garden work, and a gigantic pot filled with all different kinds of herb plants. Two days before staff leave for the summer, Alexis informs me that I must tell seven of them they will not be returning for next school year due to budget cuts. Two days later (the last day for staff), she gives me a list of another four people, and this one includes the great Spellini. He is packing his room when the Kid and I go to break the news. He puts down the box he is packing and just walks out. We have now lost the cornerstone instructional person.

Alexis gives me a copy of my final evaluation but tells me Dr. Rhoda has directed her to be sure to include the fact that my evaluations are usually late. (Oh, the lessons learned from the great Laura.) I have to do a self-reflective response and once again wonder why I just cannot be let go in peace. Dr. Rhoda has not been in my office or spoken to me in a year. She doesn't know what the kids look like or act like, nor does she know the teachers except for what she hears from the reps. Since she hasn't had Buddy to hide behind, she just hides and slides her directives under the door. For the $160,000 salary she collects and the use of the agency car, I do not know what she has contributed; and for all the out-of-state conferences she attends, I do not know of a single benefit it has rendered the Institute.

My last week there, I finally nail the Kid to the chair and go over what he must know before I leave. I notice he has a limited attention span for details and organizational reporting, but he is so technologically advanced. With a good secretary, he can delegate a lot of what I had to handle with Cruella. He leaves before I do to take a week's vacation since he will be running summer school.

With my office cleaned out, there is only one more event—Alexis's birthday. I arrange a luncheon at a local restaurant and invite all the secretaries and Evie for a girls' birthday celebration. Everyone brings presents for Alexis, and we spend more than a lunch hour celebrating. When we get back to the building, I realize there is nothing left for me to do without starting a new project I won't be there to finish. I boldly declare I will take the last two days as sick leave since I have accumulated over thirty days and know I will not be paid for them.

I go up to Alexis's office, and she is on the phone with Rodney. She waves me in, but I just wave good-bye as I leave my self-reflective response and my signed evaluation on her desk. As I walk down the sidewalk, past Rudy's grounds work, past the classroom windows, and onto the parking lot, I feel anxious that I will be stopped or sucked back in to answer one more question, decide one more room assignment, mediate one more crisis, or attend one more meeting, but I make it to my car. My heart is pounding as I pull onto the highway. A mile or so down the road, I break into a smile.

ACKNOWLEDGMENTS

To the superb team at Xlibris for their guidance, expertise and patience in smoothly navigating each step of a daunting process to make my dream a reality, I am profoundly grateful.

For inspiring and helping to craft my educational philosophy and management style and for giving me the courage to do so through their works: Jonathan Kozol, John Holt, William Glasser, M.D., Deborah Meier, Jack Welch and Dr. Wiles.

To the loved and respected people across my career whose character, integrity, passion, tireless dedication and professionalism embody the best in education; who never settled for anything less than the authenticity of connecting, in the moment, with students, I am eternally grateful:Jeannine, Patrick, John and Bill; Myra, Annie, Erin, Margit and Phyllis; Jill, the great Fantini, Mike, Donna, Julie, Boms and Fisher; Caroline, Karen, Will, Art, Robin, Aaron, JB and Ruben . . . Ruben . . . Ruben; Aileen, Virginia, Jason, Maria, Maegan, Monir and Josephine; Colleen, Sabrina, Sharon, Kim, Joanne, Cindy, Pete and Giles; Meg, Mr. Finch, Hal and Babs; Marlene, Kenny and Jonah; Judy, Russell and Larry.

To the students—every single one of you.

To my treasured grounding influence, critical eye, reality check and confidence builders: Rae Anne, Herbert, Robert, Rachael, Benjamin, Christy, Josh and Dan.

And, to a partner in every way, the love of my life and keeper of the keys to my heart, my husband Arthur; "all of this means nothing, without you."

www.ingramcontent.com/pod-product-compliance
Lightning Source LLC
Chambersburg PA
CBHW020258290526
45784CB00003B/1288